**dying
and
death**

dying and death

A Resource for Christian Reflection

Brent Waters

United Church Press
Cleveland, Ohio

United Church Press, Cleveland, Ohio 44115
©1996 by United Church Press

Biblical quotations are from the New Revised Standard Version of the Bible, © 1989 by the Division of Christian Education of the National Council of the Churches of Christ in the U.S.A., and are used by permission

Published 1996. All rights reserved

Printed in the United States of America on acid-free paper
01 00 99 98 97 96   5 4 3 2 1

Library of Congress Cataloging-in-Publication Data

Waters, Brent.
    Dying and death : a resource for Christian reflection / Brent Waters.
       p.   cm.
    Includes bibliographical references and index.
    ISBN 0-8298-1121-4 (alk. paper)
    1. Death—Religious aspects—Christianity.   I. Title.
BT825.W316   1996
236'.1—dc20   95-51680
                                                                CIP

To Diana and Erin

Contents

Preface *ix*
Acknowledgments *xiii*

Part 1 Dying, Death, and the Contemporary World

1 Overview   3
Summary and Review   23
Discussion Questions   23

Part 2 A Theological Framework

2 Changing Christian Attitudes toward
   Dying and Death   27
3 Theological Themes   41
Summary and Review   62
Discussion Questions   62

Part 3 *Moral Concerns*

4 Approaches to Moral Reflection and Discernment	65
5 Moral Questions Raised by Dying and Death	85
Summary and Review	101
Discussion Questions	102

Part 4 *Toward a Doxology of Death*

6 Epilogue	107
Appendix 1 Resolution	117
Appendix 2 Glossary	123
Appendix 3 Resources	127
Notes	*133*
Bibliography	*143*
Index	*147*

Preface

When and how one should die are poignant and divisive issues. The advent of modern medical technologies gives us greater control over the time and means of a person's death. Although many persons have had their lives extended in meaningful ways, others have had their suffering prolonged to delay an inevitable death. Caring for the dying in our society is a mixture of blessing and agony. We are uncertain whether our medical knowledge and skill are always accompanied by a requisite moral and spiritual wisdom.

Dying and death are both personal and social issues. Each of us may face such questions as: Will I face my impending death fearfully or courageously? While dying, what can I expect of friends, family, health care professionals, and the church? What in turn do friends, family, health care professionals, and the church expect of me? How much control can or should I exercise over my medical treatment? These are also questions we may ask in regard to a dying friend, a member of the family, a patient, or a parishioner.

We also face many urgent questions as a society: What are the institutional and professional duties of those who provide care for the dying? With our limited and costly medical resources, should every means of prolonging life always be employed? Who should pay the costs?

One's own death, however, is not just a personal, social, or political issue. There are closely related dimensions of what it now means to experience a good death. Dying and death are accompanied by profound theological and moral considerations. As Christians we are called to ponder and discern how we are both to live and to die faithfully. Within the community of faith, what is our mission and ministry to the dying and to those who provide their care?

Responding to this need for theological and moral reflection, several resolutions on dying and death have been introduced in recent General Synods of the United Church of Christ.[1] What you will read is a response to the church's expectation that it "offer love, compassion, and understanding to those who are faced with difficult life-ending decisions."[2]

This book is not official policy or teaching of the United Church of Christ, however, nor does it presume to dictate what Christians should believe about dying and death. It is instead an invitation to study, discuss, and discern how we might give a wise and responsible witness to our faith in the face of death. In short, this book is literally a theological resource, written for Christians who do not need to be told *what* to think about dying and death but can perhaps benefit from some assistance in *how* to think about this issue.

Nor is this a text for professional theologians and ethicists. It is intended to be used primarily by local congregations to examine dying and death in an open and honest manner. The discussion questions that conclude the parts are designed with congregational settings in mind and are meant to initiate rather than limit or confine conversation and dialogue. It is not presumed that a congregation discussing this topic will achieve any consensus. It is assumed, however, that the issues of dying and death must not be ignored or avoided by Christians, but should be explored and understood in light of God's good gifts of faith, hope, and love.

The scope of this book is not intended to be comprehensive. Many aspects of the contemporary experience of dying and death are not discussed. Legal and social policy issues, for example, are alluded to but not addressed. Such omissions are not meant to suggest that these are unimportant concerns, but rather to reflect my belief that discussion about dying and death within Christian communities should focus primarily on theological and moral questions. The agenda of the church, particularly in regard to its ministry to the dying, suffers when it is set or constrained by the laws and politics of our present age.

Some brief mention should also be made of three characteristics of the book that some readers may find puzzling, perhaps even troubling. First, there are within Christian theological and moral traditions conflicting and contradictory teachings on various topics relating to dying and death. I make no attempt to resolve these tensions. I do not presume that these disputes, which are in some cases centuries-old, can be resolved in this book. Furthermore, I believe that Christian reflection and discernment are at their best when conducted with full acknowledgment of the tensions that have shaped our faith, not when these tensions are ignored or disregarded.

Second, I have also used traditional theological language whenever possible. Given that we live in an age when such words as "sin" and "redemption" are not routinely invoked in public discussions about dying and death, this may seem a surprising tack to take. Yet I believe it is crucial for us, as Christians thinking about dying and death, to use the vocabulary from the tradition that has shaped our faith. The words we use form our perceptions, understanding, and actions. If we come to believe that certain theological terms are no longer usable or useful, we must be clear about why we are rejecting them and why the alternatives are preferable. In short, I think it is beneficial for Christian communities to struggle with the words they use, or do not use, to describe the reality of dying and death in our world.

Third, it is my intent to make the tone of this book conversational. I do not think, however, that conversation is advanced if an author implies, "I will not reveal what I believe about this topic. Now what do you, the reader, think?" I do not pretend to be objective about the theological and moral dimensions of dying and death. My beliefs and convictions have shaped my selection of topics as well as their description and presentation.

Although I have not forcefully argued in favor of particular positions, neither have I tried to disguise my own sentiments. I am convinced that such an approach is well suited to encourage genuine conversation and dialogue. If readers are both pleased and annoyed by what I have written, the purpose of this book will have been accomplished.

Acknowledgments

Although writing demands solitude, preparing to write requires fellowship. I am indebted to many individuals who helped prepare this book. Joy Skeel served as a principal consultant. Her extensive knowledge of bioethics, medicine, and theology proved invaluable. Verlyn Barker shepherded this project literally from beginning to end. He wisely knows when to push and when to give some slack to an author. The members of the United Church of Christ Working Group on Science and Technology, as well as a number of other readers, offered many helpful suggestions and criticisms of the outline and various drafts. I also greatly benefited from discussions with selected group of faculty colleagues at the University of Redlands. To list all the names and express adequately my gratitude for their time and kindness would require a preface too long for any reasonable editor to approve.

Much of the writing of this book was accomplished while I was on study-leave. I am indebted to James R. Appleton, President of the University of Redlands, for granting me the time to neglect my duties as chaplain so I could concentrate on this project. I am also very grateful to Principal Ralph Waller and the fellows and librarians of Manchester College, Oxford, for providing an ideal environment for sustained but leisurely study, reflection, discussion, and writing.

I also greatly appreciate the grace and understanding of my wife, Diana, and daughter, Erin, as I pondered and struggled with a topic that does not easily lend itself to casual conversation around the dinner table. The most valuable lesson I have learned from all these kind and generous people, however, is that it is through our friendships in Christ that the fear and sting of death lose their grip upon our lives.

Part 1

Dying, Death, and the Contemporary World

Every day one sees news stories about persons facing death. There are reports of doctors helping terminally ill patients commit suicide, of individuals who kill their dying spouses to prevent further pain or suffering, of court cases to determine whether tubes providing nutrition and hydration to a person in a persistent vegetative state should be removed, and of individuals who refuse medical treatment to allow their terminal condition to run its course. In an age when many persons are not certain whether medical technologies prolong life or delay death, such words and phrases as "euthanasia," "living wills," "death with dignity," "hospice," "advance directives," "durable power of attorney," "right to die," and "physician-assisted suicide" have become part of our common vocabulary.

Each year millions of people face the prospect of an impending death, whether their own or that of a friend or family member. Countless moral decisions must be made, particularly in light of the sophisticated medical technologies available, regarding when and how a person should die. Our present circumstances force us to consider, as individuals, as society, and as Christians, what a good death is, and what the best ways are to provide compassionate care for the dying.

The church must openly and honestly address the issues of dying and death so that it may offer a redemptive and healing ministry to those who walk this treacherous valley. For Christians, death is not a topic to be ignored or dreaded. We know that the ending of our physical lives is part of our created, and therefore mortal, existence. The church understands dying and death in light of Christ's resurrection and God's good gifts of faith, hope, and love.

Part 1 provides a brief overview of our contemporary circumstances by examining some selected issues relating to dying and death. In addition, the various levels of reflection and the need for theological discernment on this topic are introduced. It should also be remembered that behind abstract theological and moral arguments, beneath the statistics and policy debates, there are people with unique stories, hopes, and dreams. As we encounter the prospect of dying and death, particularly as people of faith, we must keep before us the images of persons loved and cherished by God. Consequently, this overview begins with four stories of dying and death.

1
Overview

Four Stories of Dying and Death

An Elderly Parent

Mary is an eighty-four-year-old widow. Throughout most of her adult life she has been actively involved in her church and community, and she has a close, loving relationship with her family. With the death of her husband five years ago, however, her health began to decline and she is now in the advanced stages of rectal cancer.

Mary's cancer treatment consists of periodic hospitalizations for chemotherapy. The side effects include loss of hair and severe nausea. Although the treatments have slowed the growth of the cancer, there is little hope that it will go into remission. Elevated dosages of pain medication also make her increasingly tired and lethargic. For the past two weeks Mary has been confined to her bed, and her daily care has been provided by her children and grandchildren.

Today Mary is admitted to the hospital because of pneumonia. Her doctor informs the family that if left untreated the pneumonia could take her life in a few days, but it can be easily cured with antibiotics. Treating the pneumonia will extend Mary's life for a few weeks, possibly months, but her family then faces the prospect of providing continual care, or arranging institutional care, for the remaining period of time.

The doctor has also informed the family that he has discussed the situation with Mary. Her only response was a weak whisper, "I'm not afraid to die." The doctor admits he is not certain how to interpret her statement because he is not confident that Mary is fully informed and rational because of her medication and distress. The doctor also indicates that he is willing to use or withhold the antibiotics, and will follow whatever instructions he is given by the family. Mary's children schedule an appointment with her pastor that evening to decide whether or not to treat the pneumonia.

A Young Adult with AIDS

Steve is a young gay man with AIDS. His condition is rapidly deteriorating. His doctor informs him that from this point on little can be done except to provide comfort and alleviate as much pain as possible with medication. Although his parents have never accepted his sexual orientation or lifestyle, he would like to go home to die. They grant his request, but also insist that his companion never visit him in their home.

For Steve, this is an unreasonable and unacceptable requirement, yet the options he now faces are bleak and limited. He can choose to stay in his apartment, but he knows that his companion will not be physically or emotionally able to provide the care and support he will require. The prospect of dying in a hospital strikes him as a frightening and lonely situation he would prefer to avoid. He could, perhaps, approach a family friend or his parents' pastor to try to persuade his parents to change their minds about prohibiting visits from his companion, but he does not think this is likely. Steve is beginning to wonder if taking his own life, soon before he is too weak, might not be the best solution.

A Single Adult

Helen is a brilliant scholar and respected professor who has announced her retirement at the conclusion of the current academic year. A few weeks after making this announcement her doctor informs her that she is in the initial stage of Alzheimer's disease.

Helen has devoted her life to scholarship and teaching. She never married and has no living relatives. A reclusive personality combined with a busy routine of research, lecturing, and writing prevented her from forming any deep or sustained relationships. Although she is highly respected by her students and colleagues, she does not have any close personal friends.

The doctor's diagnosis has left Helen both frightened and angry. She is appalled at the prospect of losing her mental capabilities, and would be ashamed if any of her colleagues should see her in such a state. She is also horrified by the likelihood of growing increasingly dependent upon other people to provide her daily care. For Helen, losing her mental and emotional independence is a repugnant fate, one that she would like to avoid.

Helen has decided to ask her doctor to help her commit "a quick and painless suicide" at a time and place of her own choosing. If the doctor refuses, Helen will ask her to recommend another physician who would be "open to my request for a dignified and merciful death."

A Spouse

Bob usually takes one of his teenage children with him when he visits his wife, Ann, in the rest home. Today, however, he wants to be alone with her. It is their twentieth wedding anniversary. As usual, he holds her hand, gently strokes her hair, and talks about a wide variety of subjects; anything that comes to mind. When he leaves, he gently kisses her cheek, and tears fill his eyes. "How much longer must this go on?" Bob wonders.

It has been over two years since Ann suffered massive head injuries in a car accident. She is now in what the doctors call a "persistent vegetative state." Her brain, except for the stem, is "dead." Since Ann is unconscious, it is believed that she is not suffering any pain, nor is she aware of her surroundings or condition. She breathes on her own, and her vital organs are functioning without artificial assistance. She receives nutrition and hydration through tubes attached to her stomach.

The doctors have informed Bob that there are no known recoveries from this condition and that as long as Ann receives nutrition and hydration she could continue to live for years. Bob has asked the doctors to remove the tubes to allow his wife to die. They have agreed not to intervene if Ann develops a life-threatening condition, such as an infection or heart attack, but they refuse to remove the tubes because it is an "illegal and immoral request to kill a patient." In addition, a court injunction prohibits Bob from removing his wife from the rest home because his intent would be to kill her by withdrawing her sources of nutrition and hydration.

Bob has had many long and bitter conversations with his pastor regarding Ann's condition. He "knows" that she would not want to be "kept alive as a vegetable." Bob does not understand why "they will not allow God to call Ann home." This evening he will meet with a lawyer to draft a petition requesting that the court allow him to have the tubes withdrawn. If the court fails him, he may take matters into his own hands to "free Ann and our family from this living hell."

Contemporary Circumstances and Issues

These four stories reflect some of the concerns associated with dying and death in our contemporary world. What now needs to be examined are the personal, social, and medical circumstances that produced these stories, as well as the theological and moral issues that accompany them.

Changing Attitudes toward Dying and Death

Today when people are asked how they would like to die, the usual response is to wish for a quick and painless death, ideally while one is asleep. This has not always been the case. Previous generations wished for a slow and lingering death so they could make their peace and say farewell to friends and relatives. There is, for instance, a petition from a prayer that asks "from dying suddenly and unprepared, good Lord, deliver us." Or as David C. Thomasma and Glenn C. Graber have written:

> In ancient, medieval, and even modern times, most persons were able to "sense" that they were dying. At that time, they would assemble their families and friends for some last words.... They kept vigil around the dying person to assure him or her that the community support they had enjoyed through life was maintained.[1]

Consequently, death usually occurred in the home, and primary care and comfort of the dying was provided by the family.

Today the situation is quite different. It is estimated that 70 percent of all deaths now occur in hospitals or other health care institutions. Medical professionals, rather than friends or relatives, provide primary care and comfort to the dying. The process of dying itself has changed dramatically. In the past, dying was a relatively brief experience; now death is often stretched out over a lengthy period of time. Sophisticated medical technologies can keep a patient alive despite the failure of vital organs, or experimental procedures can delay death. As Thomasma and Graber have observed: "People die in pieces."[2]

Society has not resolved how death should be understood or comprehended. On the one hand we often treat it as a cruel fate. We wage war against death, arming ourselves with medical arsenals to delay the inevitable victory of terminal disease. Yet on the other hand we accept death as a natural part of the human life cycle. We search for ways to help people die in a humane and compassionate manner.

Consequently, our society is simultaneously committed to fending off and embracing the inevitable reality of death. There are large investments in technologies and experimental procedures designed to prolong life. Modern medicine is often transformed into an idolatry of technology in which the purpose of life may get lost in a maze of sophisticated treatments and procedures. Yet we also search for ways to escape the dilemma of being kept alive too long. Although we may want to die quickly and painlessly in our sleep, that goal is often not achieved and is frequently a result more of luck than of planning.

Changing Definitions of Death

Determining when death occurs has changed over time. In an earlier age it was assumed that each body was inhabited by a soul or "vital spirit." A person was dead when the signs of the soul or spirit, such as breath or a pulse, were no longer present. This is why, for instance, a mirror was often held up against the nose and mouth of a dying person to look for any foggy evidence of life.

Throughout the nineteenth century and much of the twentieth death was defined in terms of the heart and lungs: "In the past death meant, clinically, the irreparable cessation of spontaneous cardiac activity and spontaneous respiratory activity."[3] A person was not declared dead until the physician verified, usually with the assistance of a stethoscope, that the heart and lungs were no longer functioning.

Yet over the past few decades advances in medicine created an unusual and unprecedented situation. With the aid of drugs, various invasive techniques, electrical shocks to the heart, and a respirator, the heart and lungs could keep going after a person's brain was "dead." This raised a unique question: Could an individual without a functioning brain, but whose heart and lungs continued to work with the aid of machines, be considered alive or even a person?

The resulting moral debates over when or whether we should "pull the plug" helped change our perception of when death occurs. A clinical and legal death can now be declared in terms of brain function as well as cardiac or respiratory activity. When there is no brain activity, as verified by reliable monitoring devices, a person can be declared to be dead.

This redefinition of death not only created the opportunity to harvest "living" organs and tissue to transplant in other patients, but is also forcing us to reconsider what we mean by "life." Under current conditions, a person is not pronounced dead until the entire brain has ceased to function. As long as some part of the brain is functioning, such as the brain stem in an anencephalic infant[4] or a patient in a persistent vegetative state, a person is not clinically or legally dead.

These situations raise the issue of whether our understanding or definition of death needs to be altered again. For instance, if an individual's "higher" brain or cerebral cortical functions—those parts of the brain where one's sense of consciousness, meaning, personality, and identity are formed—have been destroyed, should a person be considered alive, or to have life? There are proposals to define death as the cessation of higher or cognitive brain activity. Such proposals reflect a movement to define both death and life in terms of qualitative considerations, such as the ability to gain meaning or happiness from interactions with other people, rather than quantitative criteria, such as the measurable presence or absence of brain activity. In short, there is now a debate over whether life ends when the brain stops working, or when the qualities characterizing who we are as persons are absent.

Contemporary Medical Practice

Physicians care for terminally ill patients in the context of many different and often conflicting expectations. For example, William F. May has identified three primary responses to disease and death:

> (1) we respond to death with awe, a reflex that includes both fear and a shy, almost loving embrace of the event; (2) we react to death by waging an all-out fight against it; (3) we fall into patterns of avoidance and denial.[5]

According to May, these basic responses form our, as well as our physicians', expectations of how dying patients and their illnesses should be treated.

For instance, the doctor or healer may be seen as a parent and act like one: "Insofar as physicians respond to the patient's urge to avoid death, they tend to become parental figures who reassure their children and shelter them from the powers that are killing them."[6] Or the healer may be perceived as a fighter who battles a powerful enemy: "Patients prize a kind of military intelligence, tactical brilliance, self-confidence, and stamina in the physician."[7] Or finally, a doctor may be expected to be a companion who helps patients "neither fight nor avoid death, but see death as 'saving moment.'"[8]

How we perceive what healing means and what the role of the healer should be largely determines how medical technologies are used in the care and treatment of the dying. If it is believed that healing is the curing of a disease or the restoration of health, then any means available to prolong life will be used. The "parent," for instance, assures the patient that everything possible is being done; the "fighter" uses experimental drugs, therapies, and surgical techniques to buy a few extra weeks or months.

If it is believed, however, that healing is relative, medical technologies are seen as death delaying rather than life prolonging. Consequently, healing for the dying patient is understood as relieving prolonged pain and suffering. The healer as "companion" may allow or even assist the patient to die in a compassionate and humane manner; death is a relief from misery.

Differing expectations of what constitutes healing make it difficult to formulate unified medical policies and principles that shape the care and treatment of the dying. For example, health care professionals and institutions must respond to patients whose expectations range from little interference with the dying process to highly complex and frequent interventions. Providing this wide range of options accounts, in part, for the high cost of medical care. It is estimated that around 15 percent of the GNP is spent on health care, a large proportion of those resources allocated for the care and treatment of persons during the last six months of life.

Beyond the costs, modern medical care also forces us to confront an expanding litany of life-and-death decisions. As patients, many of us will have to decide what type of care we want or are able to receive. Will we pursue aggressive medical treatment or allow nature to run its course?

Health care professionals face the dilemma of offering types of care and treatments that reflect the desires of patients but are, at times, in conflict with their own values. Should a doctor support or oppose the decision of a patient to withhold medical treatment of a terminal disease?

We may have to make judgments regarding the care of an incompetent family member. How would a loved one want to be treated who is in a coma, unable to make or communicate such a determination? What do we do if such a decision is in conflict with our own values and desires? How do we reconcile the conflicts of interest that may accompany the care of the dying?

As a society we need to review and formulate legal and moral codes that govern the process of dying and death in an increasingly technological context. Should every person have a right to die in a manner of his or her own choosing? Should access to medical care while dying be determined by ability to pay? Who should pay the costs of dying and death, particularly in light of the different options that are now open to us?

A Sampling of Contemporary Issues

As this brief description of contemporary medicine implies, we face a number of moral issues concerning dying and death. What follows are some selected issues that are briefly introduced at this point and examined more fully in a later chapter.

One critical issue is when, if ever, medical treatment should be withheld or withdrawn. Any medical intervention presumes an intent to benefit the patient. Yet if a particular treatment or therapy delays death while prolonging pain or suffering, is it benefiting the patient? The answer to this question is largely subjective, reflecting personal values, desires, and expectations. An appropriate response is at times difficult or impossible to determine. For example, should treatment of an infection be withheld from someone who is in the final stages of terminal cancer? Should the nasogastric tubes be removed from a person who is in a persistent vegetative state? How these questions are answered is largely shaped by determining whether these acts are beneficial or detrimental in the particular instance.

In reaction to stories of people being kept alive too long or against their wishes, there is renewed public interest in euthanasia[9]—literally translated, "a good, noble, or merciful death." Yet defining what constitutes a good death is a difficult and complex issue. Within modern ethics literature, euthanasia has come to mean "the art of putting to death persons suffering from incurable conditions or diseases."[10]

Euthanasia can be practiced in different forms. Active euthanasia is an action intending to cause the death of a person. A lethal injection, in what is sometimes called "mercy killing," is one example. Passive euthanasia is withholding or withdrawing medical treatment to allow a person to die. At times, passive measures may include higher dosages of pain medication that speed up the dying process. The intent, however, is to relieve pain rather than to kill the patient.

In addition, voluntary euthanasia is performed "with the fully informed consent of the patient."[11] A competent adult, for instance, may request that no "heroic" measures be used in the treatment of his or her terminal illness. Involuntary euthanasia is performed "against the will or wishes of the patient."[12] An example is the killing of mental patients by Nazi or Stalinist regimes as part of their national "health policies." Nonvoluntary euthanasia is performed "without the consent of the patient, in circumstances where the patient isn't able either to give or to withhold consent"[13]—for instance, persons in a persistent vegetative state.

It must be stressed that at present euthanasic practices are legally confined to passive and voluntary techniques. Recent debates have focused primarily on issues relating to passive nonvoluntary methods. There are, however, controversial proposals to allow active voluntary and nonvoluntary euthanasia. There are few, if any, serious proposals to institute programs of active involuntary euthanasia.

Much of the controversy surrounding euthanasia reflects two

moral concerns. The first concern involves personal autonomy and informed consent. Recent trends in medical care stress the primacy of personal autonomy. Competent patients have the right to be fully informed about the state of their ill health and available therapies so they may determine whether and how their illnesses or injuries should be treated. These principles also apply in cases of terminal illness. An individual with cancer, for instance, has the right to refuse chemotherapy even if such a decision may shorten his or her life.

The more pressing dilemma is how to treat individuals who can neither assert their autonomy nor be fully informed, as in the case of infants, or adults with severe dementia or in a persistent vegetative state. In such circumstances should a surrogate, such as a relative or a friend, be assigned to make decisions regarding treatment? A surrogate could, for instance, authorize passive euthanasia on behalf of the patient. Or in cases where autonomy and fully informed consent cannot be exercised, does society have a compelling interest in prolonging life? From this latter perspective, when the wishes of an individual are not or cannot be known, it is argued that the state should act as a surrogate with a duty to preserve and protect the life of its citizens for as long as possible.

The second concern is whether or not euthanasia should be available to patients who are not terminally ill. Suppose, for example, that a young man suffers severe and permanent paralysis from a skiing accident. With minimal medical assistance this person can continue to live for many years, but he believes that a life of greatly restricted mobility and extreme dependence on other people is without value. In such a case should a request to discontinue medical assistance or help in committing suicide be honored?

The issue here is whether a person who is not dying but no longer finds life worth living has the right to authorize passive or active forms of voluntary euthanasia, or request assistance in committing suicide. On the one hand it is argued that the principles of autonomy and informed consent grant individuals the right to end their own lives. In this view it would be cruel to compel a person to continue to live a life that she or he judges to have little or no meaning or value. On the other hand it is argued that society has a compelling interest to protect and preserve life, particularly of individuals who are not dying. In short, the state has a right, if not an obligation, to prevent suicide.

A closely related issue is physician-assisted suicide. Some patients ask their doctors to help them take their own lives to stop the pain and suffering of a terminal or debilitating illness. The dramatic news stories concerning Doctor Jack Kevorkian and Timothy Quill have catapulted the prospect of physician-assisted suicide into a highly public and controversial moral arena. What is at stake is whether a doctor who helps a patient commit suicide violates a professional oath to "do no harm." Traditionally it was assumed that any action to aid the taking of a life also harmed the patient.[14] Consequently, physicians were required to do everything in their power to prolong the lives of their patients.

Advocates of physician-assisted suicide, however, claim that refusing a reasonable and fully informed request to help end a life inflicts more harm to a patient by prolonging needless agony. It is argued that under conditions of severe and uncontrollable pain or suffering the most compassionate and merciful response by a doctor is to help a patient end his or her life. Consequently, physician-assisted suicide should be understood as a rare, but needed, medical procedure similar to voluntary euthanasia.

Opponents counter that physician-assisted suicide is not a form of euthanasia: "Suicide differs from euthanasia in that the act of bringing on death is performed by the patient, not the physician."[15] What is important is the intent of the physician. For example, when a physician prescribes increased doses of pain medication knowing that it will speed up the dying process, the purpose is to relieve pain rather than cause death. If doctors actively participate in or aid suicides, it is argued, this will jeopardize the relationship of trust between physicians and patients.

Much of the controversy surrounding these issues relating to dying and death reflects differing and often conflicting views on how human life should be valued. Some individuals base their moral decisions on what may be described as a sanctity of life perspective; others stress what may be called quality of life considerations.

A sanctity of life position is based on the belief that human life is sacred.[16] From a religious perspective this belief is reflected in such a phrase as "life is a gift from God," or in secular expressions such as "life is the highest value" or an "inalienable right." In this view, the life of a healthy adult and that of a person in a persistent vegetative state are of equal value, and all available medical means should be used to protect and preserve either life. Life-sustaining medical treatments should never be withdrawn or withheld, euthanasia should not be practiced or should at least be confined to a restricted range of voluntary and passive measures, and suicide (physician-assisted or otherwise) is never permissible, for it presumes upon the prerogatives of the source or sources that give human life its sacred status.

The quality of life position is based on the belief that the value of human life depends on the judgments, desires, and preferences as assigned by individuals or their surrogates. From a religious perspective this belief is embodied in the phrase "being good stewards of God's gift of life"; a secular viewpoint is expressed in such popular slogans as "the right to die" or "death with dignity." Medicine should be used to help make an individual's life worthwhile, and a point may be reached where a person's condition becomes "so burdened or compromised that continued existence itself may be too onerous."[17] Deciding to withhold or withdraw medical treatment should be based on whether or not it enhances the quality of a patient's life. Consequently, voluntary and nonvoluntary, as well as passive and active, forms of euthanasia provide compassionate care for the dying, and physician-assisted suicide may be a legitimate option when available therapies fail to relieve prolonged pain and suffering.

What these selected issues reflect is not only the power of medicine to shape the contemporary character of dying and death, but also differing attitudes regarding how life should be understood and honored. What these issues also pose are theological and moral questions concerning the extent to which we should attempt to control the time and means of death.

Levels of Reflection

How we address these concerns relating to dying and death is, in the words of Courtney S. Campbell, "a sign of a deeper crisis of meaning in our culture. The society seems impoverished when assessing the significance of suffering, dying, and death as part of a whole human life."[18] Finding meaning for our lives in the face of suffering, dying, and death requires, in turn, various levels of reflection.

Personal

At some point many of us will be aware of our own imminent deaths. We may have to decide which medical therapies will be used to treat a terminal illness or debilitating injury. Will we, for instance, pursue aggressive treatment where the primary consideration is longevity, or will our principal objective be to control or alleviate pain even though such a strategy may shorten our lives? How we choose will reflect our deepest values, beliefs, and convictions about what makes life meaningful and significant.

In the stories of Steve and Helen at the beginning of this chapter we see the lonely and agonizing dimensions of this level of personal reflection. The options open to Steve seem equally repugnant. What overriding values and considerations should shape his final decision? For Helen, the prospect of losing her mental capability and having to depend on other people is more to be feared than death. Yet she must also ponder whether suicide is a rational response to her condition, particularly since she will depend upon her doctor to make her death quick and painless, as well as merciful and dignified. Are there other values, beliefs, and convictions that Steve and Helen should consider before making their decisions?

Family

Some day we may be called to care for a dying family member. This may require providing emotional and spiritual support for the decisions they make. Or we may have to make life-and-death determinations on behalf of a relative who is no longer able to make his or her own decisions. In addition, we may need to redefine our relationships with loved ones as we approach our own deaths. It is often with the help of a loving family that we find the strength and capacity to endure the physical, emotional, and spiritual suffering that often accompanies dying and death.

Consequently, a family often plays a central role in the dying and death process. Yet it is a role that brings with it crucial moral and religious concerns. There are, for instance, questions of honesty and promise-keeping. Should an aging and distressed parent be told everything about his or her condition, and should families be expected to keep promises regarding the treatment of a loved one if the requests prove unreasonable or highly burdensome? There are also questions of expectations and compassion. Should a family expect and encourage a relative to wage a battle against death for as long as possible? Or, in turn, should a person continue to receive every available treatment even when it becomes a heavy economic and emotional hardship for the family? In short, what duties and obligations are required of families, and what duties and obligations do patients owe to their families?

The stories of Mary and Bob illustrate some of the concerns faced by families. For example, what directions should Mary's family give to her doctor if they discover that the type of treatment their mother would want is not compatible with their own values, desires, and wishes? If Bob decides that the most compassionate thing he can do for Ann is to end her life, what effects will his action have on his teenage children?

Friends

Friends can also play an important role in caring for the dying. Loving friendships can fill a void if there is no family, or if a dying person is estranged from his or her relatives. Or friends can supplement and complement the efforts of a family while in turn giving them emotional, spiritual, and practical support.

For example, in the story of Steve should a family friend try to persuade his parents to change their minds about prohibiting any visits from his companion? Or would such an act be unwarranted meddling in a family's privacy? One could also speculate whether Helen's fears regarding Alzheimer's disease might be different if she had a close and trusted friend. Or, given Helen's sense of privacy and individual autonomy, would such a friend make any difference?

Health Care Professionals

Health care professionals play an obviously crucial role in caring for the dying. Not only do they lend necessary medical skills, but they express a "moral commitment to care for the ill."[19] They must balance their professional judgment, expertise, and values with those of their patients. They must also find fitting ways to provide compassionate care through the healing role of parent, fighter, or companion. Most important, health care professionals enter into a covenant of trust and honesty with their patients. They expect their patients to openly and honestly describe their symptoms and expectations so that appropriate care can be given.

Patients in turn enter into a covenant of trust and honesty with the professionals who provide their medical care. Dying patients, or their surrogates, expect that their illness and options for treatment will be truthfully and fully described. Most important, it is assumed they will not be abandoned while dying. The relationship between a patient and health care professionals is more than a contract where payment is made for services rendered. It is a covenant of mutual trust and loyalty: "The doctor offers a patient not simply proficiency and diagnostic accuracy but also fidelity."[20]

The stories of Mary and Helen illustrate some of the moral questions and concerns that accompany this covenant. Should Mary's doctor trust that her family has her best interests at heart, or are there reasons to suspect sinister motives? How should Helen's physician respond to her request for assistance in her suicide? Would agreeing to her request be an act of compassion? Or should a doctor refuse to take a life under any circumstances? Should Helen place a health care professional in such a quandary?

Institutions

Institutions providing care for the dying have a number of responsibilities. They are obliged to provide their patients with suitable diagnostic and therapeutic technologies, as well as ensuring safe and adequately staffed facilities. Patients in turn expect they will be treated in a fair, compassionate, and humane manner. In addition, health care institutions have a duty to society that financial resources will be managed wisely and medical resources allocated justly. Society also expects these institutions to conduct themselves in a manner that complies with legal and professional codes governing the care of the dying.

Often, however, there is a conflict of interests between dying patients and society regarding the cost of providing technologically sophisticated and labor-intensive care. Moral dilemmas arise when trying to balance the expectations of individuals and society. Some patients, for instance, insist that everything that can be done should be done, yet there are also social and political pressures to contain costs. Or at times ethical problems are created when legal and professional codes do not keep pace with changes in medical technology. It is difficult to let people die when we are no longer certain what divides ordinary from heroic measures.

In the story of Tom and Ann, personal desires collide with institutional policies. Tom wants his wife to be allowed to die. Yet it is unknown when this will occur as long as the tubes providing nutrition and hydration remain attached. Tom does not understand why an institution would fail to do what he "knows" Ann would desire. For institutions, however, there are other issues at stake. Does the removal of nasogastric tubes represent the withdrawing of a "heroic" treatment, or is the provision of nutrition and hydration part of routine medical care that should always be provided? In the eyes of the law would their removal be an act of mercy or of murder? What are the benefits and burdens to Ann, particularly since a person in a persistent vegetative state does not, to the best of our knowledge, experience pain or suffering?

The Church

Part of the mission and ministry of the church is to be present to the dying. Despite the tendency in our culture to isolate "terminal patients," the church helps ensure "that illness does not quarantine a person from the human community."[21] The church's presence occurs at a variety of levels. Pastoral care is provided to dying persons as well as to families, friends, and health care professionals. In addition, the church may establish medical institutions or attempt to influence legislation to govern health care in general and the care of the dying in particular. It should also be stressed that these various levels of ministry are not confined to ordained clergy but include laity as well.

In the stories of Mary and Bob and Ann, families turn to pastors for counsel. A number of moral questions and concerns arise in this provision of pastoral care. For instance, is the primary role of the minister to help individuals clarify their values and to support any decision they might make? Or should ministers be advocates for theological doctrines and normative values regarding a Christian understanding of life and death? More important, how do the religious faith, beliefs, and convictions of all the persons in each story shape their understanding and response to the situations of dying and death that they face?

Theological Reflection

As Christians we need to reflect together on the theological significance of dying and death. Such reflection is not confined to our own personal deaths but includes families, friendships, health care professionals, institutions, societal norms, and the life of the church. Dying and death, after all, are not isolated phenomena but affect and involve larger relationships, communities, and affiliations. Without such theological reflection the mission and ministry of the church is impoverished and incomplete.

It is ironic that the inevitable realities of dying and death are often ignored in the life of the contemporary church. Except at a funeral, death is rarely mentioned during regular services or other gatherings, and the dying are usually absent since they are largely confined to their homes or institutions. Liturgies, sermons, and educational programs often ignore these topics except for occasional allusions to our hope in the resurrection or eternal life. The realities of dying and death within the context of our contemporary age are usually not addressed in a direct and sustained manner.

In Part 2 a more detailed theological framework regarding dying and death is presented. At this point, however, some selected themes can be introduced.

For Christians the Bible is the primary resource for theological reflection. In shaping our life of faith, biblical themes mold our understanding of the significance and meaning of dying and death. For example, how does Paul's teaching that death is the "final enemy" but the grave no longer has its victory inform our attitudes concerning an imminent death? Do we face the end of life with fear, dread, expectation, or hope?

The theological traditions of the church are also resources for reflection. Theology is a critical account of faith in light of present circumstances. For instance, how does our belief that God is both the creator and redeemer of life (or the beginning and end of life) shape our understanding of death, particularly as we are able to exert greater control over its timing and processes?

The faith of the church is also a resource for shaping our moral conduct in the face of dying and death. The moral decisions we make regarding our own treatment or the treatment of others while dying are shaped by the practice of lifelong virtues or habits. For example, do the acts or deeds of Jesus (or the disciples) in light of his own imminent suffering, dying, and death provide a model for our conduct when facing an impending death?

As discussed in Part 2, these theological resources can help us formulate a fitting Christian understanding of and response to such considerations as illness and disability, pain and suffering, and the ends or purpose of human life. Most important, our theological reflection together as communities of faith will remind us that as Christians we not only seek an opportunity to "die well," but we are also called to live a good and faithful life that ends in a good and faithful death.

Part 1 Summary and Review

The purpose of this opening chapter was to provide a brief overview of dying and death in our society. We began with four stories: that of an elderly parent, a young adult with AIDS, a single adult, and a spouse. Each of these stories presented some concerns or problems associated with the process of dying and death.

The contemporary medical circumstances and social issues which helped create these stories were then examined briefly. Changing attitudes and definitions of death, as well as contemporary medical practice, have raised crucial ethical issues. The issues examined included withholding and withdrawing medical treatment, euthanasia, physician-assisted suicide, and differences between the "sanctity of life" and "quality of life" perspectives.

In examining these concerns, different levels of reflection were considered. These levels included personal, family, friends, health care professionals, institutions, and the church. Greater theological reflection within the church is also needed to envision a Christian understanding of what a good and faithful death might mean. Consequently, this chapter laid a foundation for beginning this theological reflection in the following chapters.

Part 1 Discussion Questions

1. Recall for a moment the death of a friend or loved one. What are your dominant impressions of the experience? What were your principal concerns, worries, or misgivings?

2. Review briefly the stories of Mary, Steve, Helen, and Bob and Ann that appeared at the beginning of chapter 1. What advice or counsel would you offer to any or all of the characters in these

stories? Why? How would your advice differ if you were a pastor, family member, friend, doctor, or nurse?

3. Think for a moment about your own death. What are your principal hopes and fears? Are there persons with whom you have shared these hopes or fears? If not, why?

4. Identify your initial reactions to euthanasia and physician-assisted suicide as described in chapter 1. Do you tend to regard these responses to the problems, issues, and concerns associated with dying and death as troubling or as comforting? Why?

Part 2
A Theological Framework

If the church is to accomplish its mission and ministry to the dying, it must do so within a theological context. Theology is a way of thinking about and expressing our faith. Theological beliefs form our values and shape our moral acts. The fabric of theological reflection includes the Bible, doctrine, tradition, and contemporary inquiries, as well as personal and corporate forms of experience. Theological language is the proper vocabulary of Christians, for it expresses the heart and core of our faith.

Part 2 invites the reader to reflect theologically on the contemporary circumstances of dying and death described in Part 1. Chapter 2 gives a brief overview of changing Christian attitudes toward dying and death, followed in chapter 3 by a survey of selected theological themes. A review and discussion questions concludes Part 2.

2

Changing Christian Attitudes toward Dying and Death

There is no standard or universal Christian understanding of dying and death. As well as reflecting different cultures, their meaning and significance have changed over time. These changing attitudes are not only portrayed in the Bible but are also exhibited in the history of the church.

Biblical

The biblical literature was written against a backdrop of the stark reality of death.[1] Deaths from old age, illness, famine, war, murder, or execution are routinely reported, often with little or no comment. In addition, care of the dying, except for patients with "leprosy,"[2] who were exiled from the community, was a public and highly visible activity. The care of the dying was provided by family and neighbors, and members of the synagogue and early Christian congregations often visited to offer prayers for healing. Dying and death were part of the fabric of daily life, not hidden behind the walls of specialized institutions.

Suffering was also closely associated with dying and death. It was often in the context of suffering that the biblical writers pondered the theological significance of life and death. Reasons why a person suffered and died included a curse upon an evil deed, a form of expiation,[3] or God's punishment for particular sins. The Bible also suggests that suffering may be understood as divine discipline or instruction—through illness and suffering God teaches such virtues as patience, courage, and endurance. In addition, there are biblical stories that identify a demonic evil force as the source of suffering and death, and the wisdom literature concludes that they simply reflect the inscrutable will of God that cannot be fully known or understood.[4]

As recorded in the Bible, reactions to these explanations are equally varied. Some individuals, for instance, denied or fled from their plight, while others resisted with the aid of a physician or magician. Some displayed a rational resolve in the face of suffering and death, such as when Job exclaims, "The Lord gave, and the Lord has taken away; blessed be the name of the Lord."[5] Others pursued a ritual defense against disease, as when Naaman bathed in the Jordan to cure his leprosy,[6] or in the purification rites described in Leviticus.

Suffering and death are also central themes in the New Testament. Early Christians saw their own suffering, dying, and death as a means of fellowship with Christ. In "enduring suffering" and showing a "readiness to suffer,"[7] Christians not only found meaning in their own pain but also participated in Christ's crucifixion. Suffering was a test of faith that mobilized personal "powers of resistance and steadfastness."[8] Out of such testing, hope was refined, and Christians gave witness to their trust in God. The mission and ministry of the New Testament church, therefore, were largely understood as a calling to suffer with those who suffered. This suffering presence was not only a witness to God's grace but also marked the church's "solidarity with an unredeemed creation."[9]

Although no general conclusions can be drawn from the biblical narratives regarding a Christian understanding of suffering, dying, and death, some accounts are directly relevant to the concerns of this book. First, there is the issue of suicide. Robert Wennberg points out that the word "suicide" is never used in the Bible,[10] and Karl Barth observed that it is a "remarkable fact that in the Bible suicide is nowhere explicitly forbidden."[11] Yet the texts portraying acts of suicide imply some theological and moral judgments.

There are five recorded cases of suicide in the Bible.[12] Wounded during a battle, Abimelech[13] commands his armor bearer to slay him in order to "save himself from the ignominy of having it said that he was killed by a woman."[14] The text implies that his fate is a divine judgment, that "God repaid Abimelech for the crime he committed against his father in killing his seventy brothers."[15]

King Saul is wounded in battle and falls on his own sword to avoid being captured or killed by the Philistines.[16] It is not clear, however, whether Saul's act is condoned or condemned. A proper burial and ritual mourning imply that Saul fulfilled a royal duty to avoid capture and humiliation at the hands of his enemies. Yet there is also commentary that "Saul died for his unfaithfulness."[17]

After an unsuccessful coup, Zimri[18] "killed himself by sequestering himself in the king's house and setting it on fire."[19] The biblical text adds that he died "because of the sins that he committed, doing evil in the sight of the Lord."[20] Ahithophel, when his counsel to hunt David down and kill him is rejected, returns home and hangs himself[21] because "he can only expect a cruel death after David's victory."[22] His act seemingly warranted no religious or moral sanction since he was "buried in the tomb of his father,"[23] following the custom of his day.

The most famous suicide in the Bible is that of Judas Iscariot.[24] Although the details are sketchy, it is traditionally presumed that Judas hanged himself following his betrayal of Jesus. What is unclear is whether Judas' death was a deliberate act of remorse or an accident.[25] In either case, Judas became an infamous character whose death is judged to be the result of "betraying innocent blood"[26] and "the reward of his wickedness."[27]

These biblical cases do not reveal any common theological or moral judgments regarding suicide or the taking of one's own life. In the case of Ahithophel, and possibly Saul, the act is recorded with little or no commentary. In the cases of Abimelech, Zimri, Judas, and possibly Saul again, their deaths are described as fitting conclusions to lives that had usurped God's sovereignty over life. Although there is no explicit prohibition of suicide in the Bible, Wennberg has observed that "it would be a mistake to view this silence as tacit approval or indifference, especially in light of the fact that each of these suicides was the culmination of a life that had—as presented in Scripture—turned away from God."[28] But neither can biblical authority be claimed for prohibiting the taking of one's own life under certain circumstances. Wennberg concludes: "Nevertheless, it would also be a mistake to use these accounts to draw far-reaching conclusions about the moral character of suicide and euthanasia."[29]

The second set of issues concerns biblical accounts of persons who consider death as a way to avoid or seek relief from suffering. It is reported that Jonah, suffering from severe heat, prayed that God take his life, saying, "It is better for me to die than to live."[30] God does not grant his request, however, using the occasion to teach Jonah the virtues of patience and forgiveness.

In the midst of his severe physical and emotional suffering, Job's wife urges him to "Curse God, and die."[31] Whether she is suggesting suicide, a venting of personal feelings, or that cursing God will result in a quick death remains unclear. Job, however, rejects her counsel and asks: "Shall we receive the good at the hand of God, and not receive the bad?"[32]

The New Testament records no cases of individuals contemplating or using death to avoid or find release from suffering. A few comments on how some exemplary figures responded to suffering, however, are in order. In several instances Paul did nothing to avoid persecution and physical suffering that resulted from his missionary activities.[33] Paul also asked God to remove a "thorn" that "was given me in the flesh."[34] The request was denied so that Paul learned to depend upon God's grace rather than his own strength.[35] Stephen takes no action to avoid martyrdom,[36] accepting his death by stoning with only a prayer,

"Lord Jesus, receive my spirit." And of course the prime example is that of Jesus, who submits to his approaching suffering and death as doing God's will.[37]

It is difficult to draw any generalizations from the Bible regarding the use of death to avoid or find release from suffering. Although never explicitly forbidden, it was rarely practiced. God alone was presumed to have power over life and death. To interfere with the suffering associated with living and dying would be to encroach upon divine sovereignty. The appointed time of one's death should be neither hastened nor delayed, and suffering remains a part of God's inscrutable providence.

Early Church

There is little, if any, evidence suggesting that early Christians practiced suicide or euthanasia. This was due not only to the belief in God's sovereignty over life and death, but also a prohibition against taking human life. Although Augustine believed that killing was permissible under certain specified conditions, he wrote a lengthy diatribe against suicide in the *City of God*, condemning it as a sin of self-murder. Using death to avoid sin or find release from pain reflected a fundamental mistrust of God's providence.

Caring for the sick and dying was limited to providing comfort, and visits by church elders to offer prayers for healing and anointing the ill with oil.[38] In addition, the church offered formal liturgies of healing, and the oil reserved for anointing the sick was often consecrated at the Eucharist. The church recognized healing as an office of ministry, for the *Apostolic Constitutions* "provided for the ordination of exorcists and healers,"[39] but no formal assistance was offered to take or help take one's life to relieve severe pain or suffering.

Suffering played a significant role in one's piety. Through their afflictions Christians participated in the redemptive suffering of Christ. In the face of severe persecution, such as torture or execution, suffering was a mark of loyalty or fidelity to Christ.

It should not be concluded, however, that the early church believed or practiced a sanctity of life ethic. Life was a gift, and only God, as the creator of life, was sacred. The early church followed Augustine in believing that eternal life was preferable to mortal existence. Consequently, suffering and death were not portrayed as evils to be avoided at all costs. Some things, such as fidelity to Christ, were worth dying for, requiring that at times suffering and death were preferable to living. Many of the martyrs, for instance, insisted that their families be executed along with them, believing it was better that their children die rather than be reared by pagans. The early Christians did not seek suffering and death, but neither did they try to avoid them.

Medieval

Augustine's strong denunciation of suicide became the normative position of the medieval church. The practice was condemned as both sinful and unlawful, and "it was forbidden for suicides to have a Christian burial."[40] Although euthanasia was, by implication, also prohibited, there is evidence that it was used in some areas under the auspices of the church. As Kenneth Vaux has written: "Folktales from Europe, Scandinavia, and Great Britain indicate that direct euthanasia was often practiced in the chapel itself. The 'Holy Hammer,' made of stone, was kept in an old chapel in each district."[41] When needed, a village elder would crush the skull of a dying person. The practice, however, "had given way to ritual and incantation by the seventeenth century."[42]

Although suffering continued as a central characteristic of medieval piety, its social context and theological role in the life of the faithful had changed. For early Christians, suffering marked, as in the case of martyrdom, fidelity to Christ. When Christians were no longer a persecuted minority, suffering became more associated with personal introspection. Sickness was perceived as a test of faith or God's punishment for sin. Prolonged suffering prior to death was considered a blessing, for it offered individuals time to set their lives in order and prepare themselves for divine judgment and eternal life.

It is important to note that medieval papal decrees forbade the clergy and members of orders from practicing surgery. Although the church continued to operate hospitals and hospices, the administration of medical procedures, other than providing comfort, was reserved to the guilds of physicians and surgeons. It was during this time that extreme unction or "last rites" was transformed from a ministry of healing to a sacrament administered to persons facing an imminent death. The custom of offering prayers and anointing the sick with oil evolved into a formal ritual in which the priest offered petitions to God requesting that "you may restore him to the altars of your holy church with no good thing lacking for full health."[43] By the thirteenth century, however, this sacrament makes no mention of healing, and was largely reserved to dying persons for the purpose of preparing them for death. By 1551 the Council of Trent "legally made unction a service only for those in danger of death."[44] The medieval church divorced itself from healing or medicine, concentrating on helping prepare individuals for death, as well as performing the rites of burial.

Reformation

The Reformers did little to change the church's prohibition against suicide, reinforcing the traditional theological arguments against its practice. One exception, John Donne, "argued in favor of suicide as a voluntary form of euthanasia."[45]

Although few theological treatises were written on the morality of euthanasia or "mercy killing," Protestants and humanists were more tolerant of its practice. Thomas More's *Utopia*, for example, portrayed a society in which voluntary euthanasia was legally condoned, and Francis Bacon argued that physicians had a moral duty to help their patients "make a fair and easy passage from life."[46] Martin Luther hinted at the permissibility of involuntary euthanasia. In *Table Talk*, he "spoke of having recommended that a twelve-year-old congenitally abnormal boy be drowned. He explained that such a monster or idiot is only a lump of flesh, a *massa carnis*, that does not have a soul."[47]

Suffering played a diminished role in Protestant piety. Except for Anabaptists, suffering was no longer understood as a sign of fidelity to Christ, nor was the pain associated with illness and dying seen as an opportunity for spiritual introspection. Rather, pain and suffering were regarded as evils that could be overcome, or at least ameliorated, through a God-given ingenuity to exert greater control over society and nature. This was particularly true in the case of medical advances that better protected and preserved one's health. Puritan scientists, for instance, believed that sickness and death were not natural human attributes but were results of the fall. They were, through medicine, subject to correction by God that would lead to a "millennial renewal of life."[48] Samuel Hartlib claimed that "another garden will be found, whence shall be had herbs that shall preserve men not only from sickness, but from death, itself."[49] The suffering associated with illness, dying, and death was not redemptive but was a result of a fallen order from which individuals could be saved or rescued.

During this period Protestants eroded or spiritualized any remnants of healing as a ministry of the church. The clergy confined their pastoral duties to the care and cure of souls, and the physical health of parishioners was irrelevant except as a means for gaining greater spiritual advantage. In addition, in discontinuing the sacrament of unction, preparing for death became an increasingly private affair within Protestant churches. Liturgical attention focused more on the funeral and burial following death than on the process of dying. Sickness and death would eventually be overcome through God's providence and grace, but in the meantime healing and medicine, including the care of the dying, came to be regarded as a secular function rather than a ministry of the church.

Modern

Modern Christian attitudes toward dying and death were formed in response to new philosophical and theological perspectives as well as to developments in medicine. David Hume, for instance, argued that suicide was permissible because individuals have a right to do whatever they please with their lives, including voluntary termination.[50] Jeremy Bentham, an early utilitarian, maintained that overall happiness might be best promoted through selected acts of suicide and euthanasia. There was a growing philosophical shift away from condemning suicide and euthanasia as violations of divine law or rules to insisting that such decisions be based on individual rights or utilitarian principles.

At the same time, Protestant theologians continued to concentrate on spiritual concerns. The purpose of one's faith was not to explain natural phenomena, such as illness or death, but to elicit and deepen an awareness of our ultimate dependence upon God. Nor was the task of theology to formulate strict moral codes governing personal decisions and conduct. Consequently, pastoral care was largely confined to visiting the sick and dying, relieving anxiety about death, and presiding over funerals. Although few official church pronouncements or doctrines were formulated condoning suicide or euthanasia, there was a growing assumption, at least within many Protestant churches, that death was a medical problem and an issue of personal conscience rather than a topic of theological reflection within the corporate life of the church.

At the same time that Protestant pastoral care was emphasizing personal or spiritual concerns, great strides were being made in the prevention or treatment of many diseases, resulting in a decline of infant mortality and increased longevity. One unintended side effect, however, was greater pain and suffering in some cases.

Although new medical treatments enabled some individuals to survive chronic conditions and helped to prolong the life of those with terminal illnesses, often the accompanying pain could not be adequately alleviated.

Physicians pondered whether part of their moral duty to their patients included assisting an easy and painless death, despite the injunction of the Hippocratic oath to never "administer a poison to anybody when asked to do so, nor ... suggest such a course."[51] Carl F. H. Marx, for example, maintained that a doctor "is not expected to have a remedy for death but for the skillful alleviation of suffering and he should know how to apply it when all hope has departed."[52] Other physicians argued "that there is a natural right to natural death,"[53] and S. D. Williams Jr. claimed that doctors have a duty "to destroy consciousness at once and put the sufferer to a quick and painless death."[54]

In response to the prodding of leading physicians, public advocacy groups were formed to support lenient euthanasia policies. Their purpose was to lobby for legislation supporting voluntary, and primarily passive, forms of euthanasia, but they were unsuccessful in their efforts. Several leading liberal Protestants lent their support to these efforts. Harry Emerson Fosdick and Henry Sloane Coffin, for instance, were instrumental in the founding and activities of the Euthanasia Society in America throughout the 1930s and 40s. Many Roman Catholics and conservative Protestants, however, condemned these activities, at one time charging a particular petition to be "anti-God, un-American, and a menace to Veterans ... a departure from the eternal moral law."[55]

It should also be noted that growing interest in euthanasia corresponded to developments in evolutionary theory and genetic science. In the late nineteenth and early twentieth centuries it was generally believed that ill health was the result of lineage or genetic inheritance. The health of future generations could be improved if unwanted traits were prevented from being passed on, while at the same time encouraging the propagation of desirable traits through selective breeding. Although Darwin observed that "the weak members of civilized societies propagate their kind,"[56] the Social Darwinists misrepresented his work to provide a "scientific" base for moral claims that were often racist as well as intolerant of people with mental or physical disabilities. They proposed, and in some cases helped enact, eugenics laws which included involuntary sterilization and euthanasia. Medicine, it was argued, should work with nature to hasten the death of the "weak" while encouraging procreation among the "strong." The worst example was the involuntary euthanasia practices of the Nazi regime as part of their eugenics policy to create a "master race." Although proponents of voluntary euthanasia repudiated any relationship between its use and eugenics policies, the revelation of Nazi atrocities contributed to declining public support for euthanasia following World War Two.

Contemporary

Christian responses to the contemporary circumstances of dying and death described in chapter 1 vary widely. There is currently little agreement or consensus among the churches, or among Christian theologians and ethicists, regarding what constitutes a fitting response to an imminent death. Some conflicting positions on selected issues are summarized below.

Few contemporary teachings or pronouncements of churches condone suicide in general or physician-assisted suicide in particular. There is, however, a growing willingness to consider whether the taking of one's own life, assisted or not, reflects a legitimate and compassionate option for alleviating pain and suffering.

Many Roman Catholic and conservative Protestant theologians maintain that suicide under any circumstances is wrong, for it represents an encroachment upon divine sovereignty and providence. In addition, they believe physicians should not assist such efforts, for it violates their calling as healers. More moderate positions assert that although suicide is wrong, the church should react with forgiveness rather than condemnation. The commitment of the physician to prolong life is tempered by an obligation to alleviate or eliminate the pain and suffering of patients. Some liberals argue that in the face of protracted and uncontrollable pain, physicians have a duty to assist individuals to end their lives in order to stop needless suffering. Under these circumstances it is not individual suicides who should be condemned but current medical practices that perpetuate senseless agony.

The controversy surrounding euthanasia is similar to that associated with suicide but more complex. There is among the churches a universal condemnation of involuntary euthanasia in either active or passive forms. Killing or withholding life-prolonging treatments against the wishes of an individual violates the rights of a competent patient as well as the professional obligations of the physician.

Voluntary and nonvoluntary forms of euthanasia, however, elicit far less unanimity. Some theologians and ethicists adopt a rigid sanctity of life position, arguing that life, regardless of medical circumstances, should be preserved and protected. The relative quality of an individual's life is an irrelevant consideration. Consequently, no medical treatment may be used or withheld that would knowingly hasten death. Life is always preferable to death regardless of the suffering that might be involved, and the purpose of medicine is to prolong life for as long as possible.

Other theologians and ethicists argue that passive voluntary and nonvoluntary euthanasia is permissible under certain circumstances. From this perspective no active measures should be employed to hasten death, but patients and physicians are also under no obligation to prolong life through the use of extraordinary treatments. If a medical treatment would simply prolong suffering without offering a curative possibility, or would impose an undue financial or emotional burden upon a patient or family, it may be legitimately withheld. For example, a person may choose to forgo chemotherapy for terminal cancer, or antibiotics may be withheld if a comatose individual with a terminal disease develops pneumonia. The principal problem with this position is defining the difference between ordinary and extraordinary medical treatments. Is the provision of nutrition and hydration, for example, an ordinary or extraordinary treatment for persons in a persistent vegetative state? From this perspective qualitative considerations do inform a judgment of whether life is preferable to death, and the purpose of medicine to prolong life is moderated by a willingness to allow people to die in a humane manner.

Still other theologians and ethicists argue that passive and active forms of voluntary euthanasia are permissible under any circumstance. A competent individual has the right to have his or her life ended in the face of severe pain or suffering that cannot be controlled or alleviated. Passive nonvoluntary measures may also be employed under certain conditions. For instance, medical treatments may legitimately be withheld or withdrawn from unconscious individuals who have little or no likelihood for recovery, or from conscious but incompetent persons if the procedures would cause severe pain, suffering, or hardship. From this perspective, the primary purpose of medicine is to provide comfort and relief from pain and suffering rather than needlessly prolonging life or delaying death. Such medical practice is justified by the theological or moral claim that in some circumstances death may represent the most loving and compassionate response to severe and unrelenting suffering. Consequently, Christians may have a sacred duty to help individuals achieve what they judge to be a good death.

Unlike previous generations, the current generation has few theologians or ethicists who claim that suffering is a mark of Christian piety. Although how we react to our own pain or respond to the misery of others may reveal virtuous behavior, such as courage or compassion, suffering, it is claimed, has no intrinsic value. Suffering is now viewed primarily as an evil that, through medicine, should be eliminated, alleviated, or avoided. The focus of the church's ministry in this area is to help individuals, as well as their friends and families, to emotionally and spiritually cope with the suffering that may accompany dying and death.

It needs to be noted that in contemporary Christian attitudes toward dying and death, the primary debate centers on the issue of under what circumstances assisting death represents a fitting or appropriate form of medical and pastoral care. To a lesser extent, there is also debate over what role, if any, suffering should play in a life of faith. These discussions, however, are confined primarily to formal theological and moral debates and professional reflection on pastoral techniques. What is mainly missing is consideration of how healing, suffering, dying, and death may inform the larger mission and ministry of the church, particularly as reflected in its corporate and liturgical life. Chapter 3 addresses this absence.

3
Theological Themes

If the church is to recover suffering, dying, and death as significant occasions for its ministry, a perception of these events must be rooted in a theological understanding of its mission. Theology is a way to help the church discern and proclaim what the gospel or good news means in the face of these inevitable events. Or, to pose the task another way: Why are Christians called to be present to suffering, dying, and death?

Such theological reflection does not imply a normative Christian teaching or pronouncement. Rather, the delineation of selected theological themes in this chapter is intended to stimulate consideration and discussion of how the church might offer and practice its ministry in the face of suffering, dying, and death.

God

God creates life. When, as Christians, we make this affirmation we are not claiming that God, at some distant point in the past, manufactured various life-forms and sent them on their way, nor are we declaring that God directly regulates every action of all living creatures. We are affirming that God is the source of those processes which make life possible. The God whom Christians worship and serve is the *semper Creator*, an "Immanent Creator creating in and through the processes of the natural order."[1]

God's motivation and purpose for creating life is love. Yet love is never self-sufficient nor self-indulgent; rather it is a relational quality that is shared. As Colin Gunton has written, "It follows that God is love, for it is of the essence of love to exist through reciprocal giving and receiving."[2] God does not create life-in-general but works through natural and cultural processes that mold and give shape to particular expressions of life in order that the Creator, as well as creation, might have true or genuine friendship. God creates life within "a network of mutually constituting *particularities*: distinct beings who yet take the shape of their being from one another."[3] The Bible, for instance, teaches that God created the people of Israel and later the church so that God might have a means of communion with creation.

God redeems life. Although what God creates is good, it is not perfect. The freedom of creation that makes a genuinely loving fellowship with God possible also leads to sin and evil. The relationship between Creator and creation and among the creatures themselves is distorted and destructive, in need of correction or redemption. The love that creates life is also seeking to redeem it. Thus creation and redemption are integrally linked, for one cannot be accomplished without the other. To redeem is simultaneously to create, and vice versa.

A powerful theological image of God's redemptive work is healing. Through natural and historical processes, God is healing the wounds of creation. In the Hebrew Scriptures, for instance, God calls the people of Israel to a covenantal life in which both their social relationships and their use of the land and natural resources are to be governed by justice.[4] The covenant community in turn is to be a "light to the nations"[5] so that God's "salvation may reach to the end of the earth."[6]

In the Gospels it is recorded that Jesus performed acts of healing to restore people to a full life. The church, as the body of Christ, was called to bear witness to the good news that in the death and resurrection of Jesus creation was being renewed and healed,[7] and Paul reports that the gift of healing was given to the church as a mark of God's redemptive work.[8]

God sustains life. The processes that God uses to create and redeem life also provide the sources of sustenance for particular creatures. Yet God does not sustain life merely to enable the survival of a particular species. God sustains life to achieve a greater goal or purpose. The work and materials of creating and redeeming are also preserved by God so they may be consummated, completed, or made whole in a "new creation."[9] By this means, the life God sustains is also consecrated or sanctified.

This is why the church, through the power of the Holy Spirit, is to offer hospitality to the stranger and never abandon the weak or ill. Life rises above mere survival when it is most fully shared. Healing, for instance, occurs, at least partially, when the loneliness and estrangement of sickness and dying are overcome by a faithful presence. The people of God are sanctified or made holy when they accompany those who must walk in the valley of the shadow of death. Life is sustained so that, in Christ, we live in the hope of a redeemed creation that will be renewed and fully healed.

An intricate dance between life and death is required, however, if God is to redeem, sustain, and sanctify creation. The food and energy needed to sustain life are limited. Without the death or passing of the old the new cannot emerge or be created. Particular lives must end to perpetuate life-sustaining processes, for the "biological death of the individual is the prerequisite of the creativity of the biological order."[10] The stark reality of our own mortality is very much a part of our Christian faith.

The God we worship as the One who creates, redeems, and sustains life is also the author or source of suffering and death. According to Isaiah, it is God who claims that "I form light and create darkness, I make weal and create woe; I the Lord do all these things."[11] No human or earthly power can eliminate suffering or prevent death. They are inevitable realities shared by all living creatures. As Christians we do not see death as an unfair or cruel fate. Rather we affirm that Jesus Christ is "Lord of both the dead and the living."[12] Life and death characterize the creation that God is sustaining and redeeming.

Death, then, is part of God's ordering of creation. At a general level divine providence is reflected in natural processes that create and sustain life. As Creator, God is establishing an evolving order in which life is sustained through the interplay between life and death. Or, as John Polkinghorne has written: "Providence is closely assimilated to creation. Indeed it becomes the everyday experience of the creative process in a world which is sustained in being by its Creator."[13]

Yet God is not a detached observer of creation, not simply a master craftsman who fashions the universe and then stands back to admire the finished product as an "impotent spectator."[14] The God we worship is a personal God who providentially cares for the lives of individuals. If God is redeeming the world, the particular circumstances of our lives are not ignored; God hears the groaning and cries of creation and its creatures. Or again as Polkinghorne has observed; "Christian theology cannot do without a God who acts in the world by more than simply keeping it in being, for it looks to the One who brought Israel out of Egypt" and "raised Jesus from the dead."[15] We give God thanks and praise for the blessings and tender mercies we receive as expressions of God's redemptive care and love.

General and particular expressions of God's providence, however, do not explain away or eliminate the realities of suffering, dying, and death. God's ordering of creation does not spare us from evil. Indeed death itself is a central or necessary aspect of sustaining creation over time. As Christians we must honestly and frankly admit that no "account of God's action can avoid the fact of the widespread existence of evil and suffering in the world."[16]

We live in a world where the death of individuals, civilizations, and entire species occurs regularly and frequently. It is also a world where some deaths seem unfair or tragic. The death of an infant with leukemia, for instance, seems much more lamentable than the sudden and painless death of a person who has lived a long and full life. As Christians, how do we reconcile an austere God, "maker of heaven and earth,"[17] with a personal God who has numbered the hairs on our head?[18] How do we worship a God who uses the suffering and death of particular lives to create, redeem, and sustain the more general processes of life? Or to use more traditional theological language, is a seemingly indifferent Creator compatible with a personal Redeemer and Comforter as revealed in Jesus Christ and the Holy Spirit, particularly in those instances when we face the prospect of suffering, dying, and death? Before we may pursue additional reflection on this issue, however, we must first consider a theological understanding of life.

Life

In the first account of creation in Genesis animate life is a blessing from God. As opposed to lifeless objects and inanimate forms of life, only animate creatures are blessed by God and given the charge to "be fruitful and multiply."[19] In addition, humans are given dominion over creation and charged with the responsibility to tend it wisely. Although all of creation is "good," only life is blessed as a sign of the "effective action of the creator."[20] Creation itself is directed toward bringing forth and being hospitable to life.

Consequently, our lives are gifts and loans from God, not a product of our own effort or ingenuity. Our lives are not our own because their origin and destiny remain beyond our control. A fitting response, then, to the life given to us by God is thanksgiving and gratitude. We sing praises to God for continuing to bless creation with the gifts of life that are granted to us.

Although life is freely given to us by God out of divine love and grace, it is not a gift we may or should casually ignore, neglect, or discard. As John F. Kilner has observed, life is a sacred custody "entrusted to us as part of a much larger purpose God has for us."[21] To speak of life as a gift does not imply a metaphor of an ordinary Christmas or birthday present that is easily taken for granted. It is more like a treasured heirloom or inheritance that is handed over from parent to child—from generation to generation—for safekeeping. The giving and receiving of such a gift presumes high levels of trust and responsibility.

A gift and loan of life, therefore, requires stewardship. We are expected to live our lives wisely, in accordance with God's creating, redeeming, and sustaining ways and intentions. At a general level this requires responsible human conduct to ensure that natural processes remain life-sustaining rather than life-threatening, and that social institutions honor and support rather than neglect or destroy particular lives. At a personal level we become faithful custodians of life through the love, care, and compassion we share with family, friends, colleagues, and strangers.

It is also important to emphasize that we are to exercise our stewardship not as monarchs but as loving and faithful servants. We are custodians of life in the name of Christ; it is not our possession to do with as we please but a precious gift and loan entrusted to our care. We are not the lords of our lives but rather fiduciary agents or trustees.

In this role we are stewards of life not only for our own benefit, or even for the survival of the human species. Such a belief is far too narrow, for we are not entrusted with God's blessing merely to perpetuate human life. Rather, our gift and loan of life is used to serve God in sustaining life so that the work of redeeming creation might be completed. Life has a God-given purpose that we are called to attend and embrace as our own.

Such a claim for life runs counter to the secular and egocentric spirit of our age. We have come to believe that life has a purpose only to the extent that we concoct or manufacture one. Our actions are literally self-interested and self-oriented because this is the core in which we find or construct the semblance of any purpose for our lives. We have been led to believe that we are self-constructed creatures. In a corruption of the old Westminster shorter catechism, the end of life becomes loving oneself and enjoying oneself for as long as possible.

From a Christian perspective, however, this process is backwards. It is God, not we, who bestows our lives with their purpose. God creates and sustains both life and death so that creation is drawn toward its redemption. As Colin Gunton puts it, "Creation was not simply the making of the world out of nothing, not even that world continually upheld by the providence of God, but the making of a world destined for perfection, completedness."[22] Particular creatures participate in this movement toward the world's salvation by fulfilling the purposes for which they were created. Human beings, for instance, strive as stewards of the gift of life to mark their faithful dominion over a creation that is heading toward its final transformation as a new creation in Christ. Gunton has observed: "Those who first proclaimed that the chief end of man is to glorify God and enjoy him for ever enunciated a profound truth."[23]

In order to be faithful caretakers of the gift and loan of life, the purpose and ends of our lives must be formed or shaped by God. We are to be conformed to Christ rather than the world.[24] Such faithful stewardship, however, is based on love, grace, and obedience, a perfect communion and friendship with God in order that all creation might be sustained and transformed. Obviously such perfect communion does not accurately characterize our current circumstances, for our lives and world are tortured by sin and suffering. Consequently, we must turn our attention toward what the redemption of creation might mean.

The Redemption of Creation

As Christians we confess that our lives are distorted by sin. The life God has created is also in need of divine redemption. Sin is a disordering of creation, similar to a pervasive sickness in which the symptoms have become so common they are difficult to diagnose but the disease nonetheless continues to destroy the patient. In its most extreme form, sin is a refusal to accept our stewardship of the gift and loan of life. It is a toxic rather than nourishing orientation that leads to a "deathwards direction of life."[25]

Redemption or salvation reorients us and enables us to become faithful custodians of life. A variety of metaphors and images in the Bible portray this *metanoia*, or transformation. For instance, we are spared God's judgment,[26] become "born from above,"[27] are chosen to be a "holy priesthood,"[28] are forged into a "new creation,"[29] and made "holy and acceptable to God."[30] The common thread in these images is that in Christ sin is conquered, and creation finds the source of its redemption and transformation. In the life, death, and resurrection of Jesus Christ, the orientation of the world is changed from deathwards to lifewards.

This renewing of life in Christ occurs at both general and particular levels. In the first instance, all of creation is being redeemed by God. As Paul instructed the church at Rome, "creation waits with eager longing"[31] to be redeemed from its "futility."[32] The natural world is not simply a background against which the drama of saving human souls or human history is played out. Rather, the entire created order is the object of God's saving acts, for "redemption is what God has done for the whole."[33] The world must be reordered and renewed so that creation may be freed from its futility and "restored to its proper function as the environment for God's restored children."[34]

It is within this larger context that we must understand our own particular or personal redemption. Our lives, especially their beginning and end, are elements within God's greater work. The world is not something from which we are rescued; our "salvation takes place *within* the created and natural order."[35] There is no Christian theology of disembodied salvation. Our redemption is integrally linked with God's creative and sustaining action upon a material reality. Again, as Paul reminds us, we, along with creation, "groan inwardly while we wait for adoption, for the redemption of our bodies."[36] We wait not to be rescued from our status as creatures, but for our creaturely status to be transformed and perfected by God.

As previously discussed, God's care of our lives involves suffering and death. As a result, these realities also play a role in God's redemption of life. To suggest how this can be the case, we will look briefly at how healing, suffering, and ministry can be redemptive.

Healing is redemptive when life is empowered to accomplish the purposes for which it is created. Threatened ecosystems, for example, are healed when restored or allowed to be life-sustaining. Social systems are healed when reoriented toward practices that support rather than neglect the needs of people. In both instances healing occurs when nature and history help order life in a way that supports God's creative, redemptive, sustaining, and sanctifying intentions.

Likewise, in our personal lives, we are healed when we are empowered to fulfill our purpose to enjoy and glorify God and live in communion with the Creator, creation, and the creatures. Such healing occurs at a physical level. Being cured of an illness allows us to more fully worship and glorify God and more actively serve the needs of our neighbors.

Healing also occurs in the interpersonal and spiritual dimensions of our lives, when our estrangement with others is reconciled, or we are granted a sense of peace in the midst of adversity. Whenever and wherever health is restored it should invoke in us a deep gratitude, whether its source is natural regenerative powers, medical or technical skill, or something we might call miraculous, for it redirects our strength and attention back toward the source of life.

It should not be assumed, however, that healing will always result in what we desire. For healing to be truly redemptive, we receive what we need rather than what we necessarily want. It is God's will and not our own that must be done if creation, as well as its creatures, is to be sustained and redeemed.

An example of the tension between confusing our wants with our needs, or God's will with our own, can be seen in petitionary prayer that we often associate with sickness and healing. As Christians we should pray to God requesting specific acts of healing. Yet if the results are not what we hoped or imagined, we should not conclude that God is not listening or is unsympathetic to our plight. A petition for healing is not a demand that God do what we want; rather, it seeks a conformity with God so that healing might occur within creation and our lives in ways we may not fully recognize or comprehend. As John Polkinghorne has observed, "Prayer is neither the manipulation of God nor just the illumination of our perception, but it is the alignment of our wills with his, the correlation of human desire and divine purpose."[37] Healing is not so much a matter of natural or humanly orchestrated phenomena as it is a mending of the relationship between Creator, creation, and the creatures. Polkinghorne goes on to offer the following example:

> A friend of mine was mortally ill and was given six months to live. His wife was encouraged by a wise friend to pray with her husband daily and to lay her hands upon him for healing. He died almost exactly six months to the day from the time he had received the news from his doctors. Afterwards his wife asked herself what healing he had received through her prayerful ministry. She concluded that his quiet acceptance of the destiny of imminent death (which profoundly moved many people around him) and the peacefulness of his passing (which might, in view of his disease, have been very distressing) were the healing he had received.[38]

In death there is a redemptive healing that embraces our lives.

What links various acts of healing in a redemptive manner is a profound shift in perspective or orientation. We no longer grasp at life trying to control it as a possession but treat it with the faithful respect that is due this blessing. We respond with gratitude because we have been claimed and redeemed by God. Healing begins when we can attest that our lives are not our own but belong to God. Such healing is genuinely redemptive because it directs our attention toward the same divine love and grace that are creating and sustaining the world. It is a profound reorienting of our lives where we are empowered to profess the words of John Newton's hymn: *I once was lost, but now am found/ Was blind, but now I see.*[39]

For the Christian, suffering too can be redemptive. Suffering becomes redemptive when it is used to help us glorify God or fulfill the purposes for which we are created. Such a belief runs counter to the prevalent ethos of our age which assumes that "suffering is an unqualified evil" that should be avoided or "removed at all costs."[40] Nothing good, it is often presumed, can result from suffering.

Yet, as Christians, our redemption is rooted in the suffering of Christ's cross. In Isaiah's vision it is through the "wounding" of

God's suffering servant that "we are healed."[41] Suffering is a significant dimension of our faith, for as Kilner has written: "Far from enjoying a life free of suffering, servants of Jesus in a fallen world will necessarily suffer."[42]

To believe that suffering can be redemptive, however, is not the same as believing it is good. For the Christian, suffering is neither good nor evil in and of itself. It is not an intrinsic value but an instrumental value; it is never an end in itself but may sometimes be a means to achieve what is good. We suffer in the hope that suffering may be used to accomplish a greater good. It is trusting "that God can bring good things out of bad without making the bad things themselves good."[43] Christians do not inflict needless suffering upon themselves or others as a mark or display of piety. Rather, as Stanley Hauerwas suggests, "Though suffering is not to be sought, neither is it to be avoided. Often we achieve the good only because we are willing to endure in ourselves and others an existence of suffering and pain."[44]

Within the Christian way of life there are two ways that suffering may be redemptive: when we suffer *for* others, and when we suffer *with* others. Such forms of suffering are redemptive when they follow the model set by the life and work of Jesus.

In his crucifixion Jesus suffered for others. Jesus suffered the pain and death of the cross, giving "himself for our sins"[45] as a sacrifice to redeem creation. Likewise, if our lives are to be patterned after the way of Jesus Christ, then we too must be willing, at times, to suffer for others. The cross is not confined to the distant past; its shadow extends to our day where we "are not invited now to live in the created order as though there had been no cross."[46]

One example is the suffering of childbirth. A mother accepts an inconvenient pregnancy and the physical pain of delivery so that life may be given to her child. Or we may be called to risk surgery to donate an organ to a relative, or experience the pain of having bone marrow removed to be given to a sick friend or stranger. At the end of our lives we may choose to forgo experimental medical treatments intended to extend our lives if that would spare our families financial hardship or free medical resources that could be used by others with a greater likelihood for recovery. In a variety of ways we are called to make personal sacrifices that may lead to our suffering for the sake of others. Such instances are redemptive when they give others opportunities to better accomplish their stewardship of life.

More frequently we are called to suffer with others. Once again the life and work of Jesus provide a fitting model. Jesus does not forsake those in need but heals them or seeks ways to bring them into closer communion with God and creation. The pattern that emerges from his ministry is one to be emulated by the church: The people of God do not ignore or abandon those who are suffering.

At the corporate level our suffering with others is expressed, for example, through policies and institutions which guarantee that the sick and dying will receive adequate medical care. At a personal level we share the suffering of others by being genuinely and fully—physically, emotionally, and spiritually—present. The one who is suffering, however, can still be abandoned in a room filled with people if none are truly present, willing to share the fears and hopes of the person in pain. The omnipresence of medical technology needs to be accompanied by the warm touch of a human hand.

A suffering presence is redemptive when it helps restore communion among Creator, creation, and the creatures. Suffering works its greatest evil when it is endured in lonely isolation, for life is created by God to be shared, even in the final moments before death. From a Christian perspective the worst feature of dying is not the inevitable fate of death but the prospect of making the journey alone and abandoned. Our suffering with others is redemptive when it reminds us that "we all invariably are and indeed should be at one another's mercy."[47]

The redemptive possibilities of healing and suffering intimate that the church should also offer a redemptive ministry, particularly in the context of dying and death. At its best the ministry of the church is always redemptive, for the preaching of the Word and the sacraments are powerful means for bearing witness to God's creative, redeeming, and sustaining ways in the world. Our ministry is nothing less than the reenacting of Christ's ministry, death, and resurrection in our daily lives.

Yet there is a need to lift up healing and suffering as specific foci of the church's ministry. As previously mentioned, sickness, dying, and death may be ignored by the contemporary church. Healing is relegated to the province of medical professionals, and suffering often remains hidden behind personal walls of privacy. One result is that in our most defenseless moments we are often unwittingly abandoned by the community of faith to the lonely confines of medical institutions and solitary suffering.

It is time for the church to recover, in the name of Christ, redemptive healing and suffering as central to its ministry. Such ministry should extend beyond individual pastoral care, involving both clergy and laity, to mark healing and suffering as significant dimensions of its larger mission and liturgical life.

For instance, petitionary prayers for healing should play a prominent role in worship. The purpose is not only to request that physical and spiritual health be restored, but also to ensure that a vital link is maintained between the ill and healthy through our shared life of prayer. In addition, rituals that honor those who are sick and suffering, as well as those who provide their care, need to be celebrated. These may appropriately take the form of a service of healing, including the practice of anointing the sick. Again the purpose is not to conjure a magical divine power but to faithfully align ourselves with God's redemptive intentions for creation.

Most important, the church should ensure that it suffers with those who suffer. We are called to provide a faithful and trusted presence to those who could most easily be abandoned and forgotten. At the very least this requires that, as Christians, we gather for worship and fellowship at times and places where our brothers and sisters in Christ who are sick, suffering, and dying can be included to the fullest extent of their strength and capacity. Beyond this the church must also consider how to extend its ministry, as part of its stewardship of life, to the strangers we encounter who are also in need of God's redemptive touch in the midst of their suffering and need of healing.

To reflect theologically on the redemption of life through the means of healing, suffering, and ministry, however, should not remain an abstract enterprise. It must also be pertinent to our current circumstances, showing some understanding of what suffering and dying mean in our technological age.

Suffering and Dying

For Paul, death is a consequence of sin. The creative intentions of God, he believed, did not include death but entered creation following Adam's sin as recorded in Genesis.[48] As Paul teaches, the "wages"[49] of sin are death. Accordingly, "all die in Adam,"[50] for it was because of his sin of disobedience that "death came into the world."[51] Or, as Augustine remarked, "The first men were indeed so created, that if they had not sinned, they would not have experienced any kind of death; but that, having become sinners, they were so punished with death, that whatsoever sprang from their stock should also be punished with the same death."[52] Suffering and dying are not, for Paul and Augustine, natural dimensions of God's created order but attributes of a fallen or sinful order.

The relationship between suffering and sin is played out at different levels. There is a natural suffering that is random but universal. As mortal creatures we undergo a necessary physical decaying of our bodies that makes us more susceptible to illness, pain, and distress. Each of us has unique genetic characteristics that either help protect us or make us vulnerable to life-threatening diseases. There are social, political, and economic structures as well that inflict suffering. War, poverty, and polluted air, water, and soil contribute to the process of dying. The personal decisions we make may also lead to suffering. A decision to smoke, refrain from exercise, or eat an unhealthy diet, for instance, can lead to cancer or heart disease.

The point here is not to suggest that there is a cause-and-effect relationship between sin and suffering or that suffering is a punishment for our sinful conduct. Sin is not a commodity that can be measured and apportioned. The greater the sin the worse the suffering is not a Christian or a biblical formula. Instead we find in the Bible a pondering why the "treacherous thrive"[53] while there are "righteous people who perish,"[54] as well as Jesus' declaration that God makes the "sun rise on the evil and on the good, and sends rain on the righteous and unrighteous."[55] Being free of suffering is not a reason for smug self-righteousness, nor is the suffering of others a license for moral judgment.

The reason for linking suffering with sin is to illustrate the complex nature of our current circumstances, particularly as they relate to dying and death. The relationship between sin and suffering is multifaceted, including factors both within and beyond our control; acts of commission and omission; good intentions leading to lamentable results. In the face of such uncertainty a sinful orientation is often expressed either in an attempt to do too much, or in a willingness to settle for too little.

A fitting example of this sinful tendency can, at times, be seen in the medical care of the dying. We may employ every available treatment to prolong life or delay death for as long as possible. This crusade is justified by the value we place on controlling our lives (defending our bodies against a deadly disease), and extending our longevity. These efforts may reflect well-intentioned goals, yet the unintended results can prove tragic. For the sake of exerting greater control life-sustaining technologies are used that often leave the patient with little ability to regulate his or her eventual destiny. While medical ingenuity extends the length of individual lives, the suffering of the patient, family, and friends may also be prolonged. As Hauerwas has noted, "The irony is that no one is more controlled than those who assume they are in control or desire to be in control."[56] The attempt to control the end of life by extending it may actually result in a loss of freedom.

At the other extreme we may settle for doing too little for the dying. In the face of a terminal disease, life-sustaining treatments may be withheld for fear of prolonging needless suffering and incurring exorbitant costs. This approach is condoned by appeals to allow persons to die with dignity and to prevent needless suffering. These are realistic and reasonable concerns, yet the unintended consequences can again be tragic. In the name of a dignified death or preventing needless pain the dying may be urged subtly to embrace a quicker death even though they may have the capacity to live a meaningful life in the midst of suffering. Doing less than can be done may represent an easy abandonment.

Attempting to do too much or settling for too little can be thought of as sinful because they produce concrete and evil acts, particularly in the care of the dying, that frustrate the purposes for which humans are created. We are not created either to control or to abdicate our responsibility for our lives but to exercise our stewardship of God's gift and loan of life. What doing too much or doing too little have in common is that they prevent us from embracing the redemptive healing and suffering that can accompany dying and death. This is another reason why sin is related to suffering and death. For if evil has no cause, if it just "happens," as a vulgar bumper sticker declares, then we are without hope or recourse for overcoming it. If the evils of suffering and death are rooted in sin, however, then they are subject to redemption or correction by God.

Consequently, as Christians, we do not condemn, judge, ignore, or evade the suffering of others because it is rooted in sin. Rather we are called to respond with compassion, caring, and faithful presence to those who suffer. For we are ourselves sinners who confess our sins and accept God's mercy and forgiveness.

As Christians, our compassion is unqualified and unconditional. It makes no difference whether suffering is the result of random forces or the consequence of personal decisions. We are, in a sense, indifferent to the causes of suffering, seeing only the need. We are then moved to care for the suffering out of gratitude for the love God has granted us in Christ. Our caring in turn may be demonstrated at a social level through medical institutions and practices that neither attempt too much nor settle for too little. At a personal level we are genuinely and fully present so that suffering might be shared. We are a people formed by God who willingly suffer with others and at times are able to suffer for others. Through compassion, caring, and a faithful presence we accomplish our stewardship of life by making it possible for dying and death to be accompanied by redemptive healing, suffering, and ministry.

Yet having said all this we are still confronted by a final, disturbing, and difficult question: Ultimately, what are we, as Christians, to make of death?

Death

If death, as Paul claims, is the consequence of sin, do we understand it as a friend or an enemy? There are biblical and theological precedents for both possibilities.

Paul, for instance, declares that death is the "last enemy."[57] Yet, since "death has been swallowed up in victory,"[58] he also asks rhetorically: "Where, O death, is your victory? Where, O death, is your sting?"[59] Since Christ has conquered sin there is no reason why Christians should fear death, for its dominion has been replaced by the dominion of eternal life. In a sense death becomes the means for God to deliver the promise of the new life in Christ. Augustine, for his part, wonders "whether in very truth death, which separates soul and body, is good to the good?"[60] He also finds it difficult to understand why mortal life would be preferable to eternal life which "gives true happiness."[61]

Christians may view death as both an enemy and a friend, largely depending upon the circumstances being faced. Death remains an enemy in revealing that God's redemption of creation remains incomplete. The groaning of creation's futility is not yet relieved. Death is still the most stark reminder that God's ordering of the world continues to be distorted by sin, an enemy that seeks to devour God's gift of life.

Yet on other occasions death may be a friend. Death does not separate us from the One who creates, redeems, and sanctifies us. As Christians we accept the inevitable reality of our mortality not as a divine miscarriage of justice but as part of God's ordering of creation. There is for each of us, after all, "a time to be born and a time to die."[62] As Robert Wennberg has observed, "We most certainly should affirm that a person's death ought to occur only when God decrees that it occur."[63] Particularly in the face of prolonged suffering, the time of one's death is, like life, a blessing. The challenge is how we, as mortal and sinful creatures, are to align our efforts with God so that death occurs at a proper or fitting hour and so that we may be at peace when death draws near.

This tension between death as enemy and friend sets the parameters of how we should respond and what we should try to accomplish when entering the shadow of an imminent death. As John Kilner insists: "Death is both enemy and destiny, both penalty and promise, both cross and resurrection. It is necessarily a real evil, the result of rebellion against God, but it is something over which God's love did, does, and will triumph."[64] Our death, as well as the death of others, is something to be resisted but not for too long; an occurrence we welcome but never prematurely. There is a sacred timing that should be honored in the ending of our lives.

If there is a fitting time for each to die, then any notion that death represents a medical failure must be firmly rejected. It is absurd to expect that medicine will ever prevent anyone from dying. It may delay the time of one's death, but it can achieve nothing more. Medicine can provide care and comfort to the dying by alleviating their pain, but if it wages a war against death it, and we, will always lose.

Medicine as a moral community does fail, however, when it fights too long or retreats too early. For in both cases the dying are abandoned either to the illusion of controlling their own fate, or to the expedient calculation that their lives are no longer worth preserving. If our deaths are to be timely and accompanied by redemptive healing and suffering, medicine must find a fitting balance between intervention and restraint. Our stewardship of God's gift and loan of life includes a good and faithful ending.

Although death is not a medical failure, grief is nonetheless an appropriate response. Even though death does not separate us from the love of God, our dying will be a passing; we will lose something with the ending of our mortality. In the shadow of our own impending death we may legitimately grieve for the approaching loss of friendships and loving relationships, as well as the lost opportunities to complete the tasks that will remain undone. As Christians "we must die in a way that provides for healthful and morally sound grief for those whom we leave behind."[65]

Likewise we mourn the death of friends and loved ones for the loss their deaths will leave in our lives. Genuine grief prevents us from denying the reality of death, and does not allow death to work its evil among the living. For true grief is not synonymous with fear or bitterness. We do not fear the eventual fate of those who are dying for we are confident of God's love and grace. Nor should we resent the separation from friends or loved ones, for we trust in God's care that our deaths are timely and fitting within God's creative, redemptive, and sustaining purposes.

Genuine grief is, rather, a mark of gratitude and remembrance. We give thanks to God for the gift of life that has been given to all creatures, and we remember those who have died that they may continue to be a source of strength in our lives. Grief, like healing and suffering, can be redemptive if "we die in a way that leaves behind us a morally healthy community of grief."[66] Authentic grief is literally a bittersweet experience.

Our grief can be redemptive because of the source of our hope. Put simply, our hope rests in the raising of Jesus Christ from the dead; our destiny lies "in a resurrection like his."[67] In Christ our deaths are incorporated or raised up into God's life. Paul insists that "we hope for what we do not see."[68] We are given a hope that "encourages us and sustains us by promising to our present experience, with all its ambiguity, a completion which will render it intelligible."[69] In Christ's resurrection we are given the assurance that we do not live or die in vain.

We share a general hope for all creation. We expect to be present when the groaning of creation will cease. For Christ is the firstfruit of a new and fully redeemed creation where death will be abolished.[70] We look forward to a time of a "restored creation" that lives in "conformity to the death and resurrection of Christ."[71] Death itself is embraced by a larger hope that the sin which plagues and distorts creation will be brought to a redeemed consummation or final end.

As Christians, however, we also have a particular hope. We do not see our lives being absorbed into a larger cosmic substance.

Although we are part of the larger hope for all life, it is also our unique lives which are created, redeemed, and sustained by God. We are shaped by what John Macquarrie calls "total hope,"[72] in which the contours of our particular lives make up the fabric of a larger pattern of life, or specific and valued moments "in the evolving potentiality of a universe in which chance and necessity maintain their fruitful interplay and within whose open process the immanent activity of God is at work."[73]

Yet when we claim along with Paul that our hope rests in things unseen we should be careful about what we are claiming. Our hope is not wagering that God will perform some great magic trick in the future, nor are we claiming continued individual existence or survival as a disembodied spirit. Our hope, as Christians, is something more than pulling a redeemed world out of a cosmic hat or a ghost story.

This is why, as Christians, we place our hope in resurrection rather than immortality.[74] A hope unseen is not one completely divorced from our present, embodied experience. Unlike Plato we do not believe that salvation lies in freeing a trapped soul from a mortal body. Rather we share with the Jewish faith a belief in what we may call the psychosomatic unity of life. We come to be who we are as embodied creatures. The great fear of Sheol in the Hebrew Scriptures was the "horror of the 'naked soul.' "[75] It is our entire being—soul, mind, and body—that is created, redeemed, and sustained by God. As John Polkinghorne has observed, "When we come to talk of the hope given to all humankind in Christ, we are not talking about spiritual survival but about resurrection, the reconstruction of the psychosomatic being, even if the new body is a glorified one, as Paul's phrase 'a spiritual body' (*soma pneumatikon*) suggests."[76]

The raising of Jesus from the dead is a unique event. Yet as a sign of hope it is total and complete, for it marks "an ultimate redemptive transmutation of the matter of this world, of which Jesus' resurrection was an anticipation."[77] In short, what happened to Jesus in and following his death will also, in the fullness of time, occur in ours; "for as all die in Adam, so all will be made alive in Christ."[78] Easter morning was but the firstfruits of a later harvest.

It is because of this hope that we may confess that God creates, redeems, and sustains our lives. It is in this hope that healing, suffering, and ministry can be redemptive, and where we may find the strength and capacity to offer compassion, caring, and a faithful presence in the face of dying and death. It is because of this hope that we may call death both enemy and friend, for it does not represent the victory of sin or the failure of medicine but a necessary part of God's ordering of the world toward its final end. This enables us to embrace a genuine grief, filled with gratitude and remembrance, in the face of death, as well as invoking a sacred trust and confidence in a future whose details remain unclear as "puzzling reflections in a mirror."[79]

Death is the real end of our mortality; we grieve but not forever. Because of Christ our mortal death is not the final word. Like a faithful and loving healer, God does not forsake us. This assurance is the source of our hope, and the poverty of human language cannot adequately capture or portray its breadth or depth. As John Polkinghorne so wisely reminds us: "Our ultimate hope rests in that faithfulness which will not abandon anything of value once it has come to be."[80]

As asserted earlier in the chapter, theology is the proper or formal language of the church for thinking about and expressing its faith. One way of testing the adequacy of theological reflection is to see if it makes any practical difference in our daily life and conduct. How do theological beliefs about God, life as a gift, or hope in Christ's resurrection, for instance, inform our understanding of and response to such issues as euthanasia or physician-assisted suicide? In other words, how do theological themes inform our morality? This question will be explored in Part 3, Moral Concerns.

Part 2 Summary and Review

Part 2 invited the reader to reflect theologically on the contemporary circumstances of dying and death. As reflected in the Bible, the early and medieval church, the Reformation, and modern and contemporary responses, Christian attitudes toward dying and death have changed over time. Historically no standard or universal understanding has emerged.

To recover suffering, dying, and death as a focus of its mission, the church needs to establish a theological context for its ministry. Consequently, such theological themes as God, life, redemption, suffering, dying, and death were briefly examined. These theological themes shape an understanding of life as a gift and loan. How, as Christians, we best exercise our stewardship of this gift and loan is a moral task that will be explored in Part 3.

Part 2 Discussion Questions

1. As Christians, how does our calling to "suffer for" and "suffer with" influence our attitude or perception of our own dying and death, as well as the dying and death of others?

2. Can traditional Christian teachings regarding the relationship between sin, suffering, and death be reconciled with beliefs about God's love and grace?

3. Do you think an emphasis upon God's redemption of creation rather than of individual souls provides or eliminates a source of strength, hope, and consolation in the face of an impending death? Why?

4. Given the theological themes described in Part 2, is there any additional advice or counsel you would care to offer to any or all of the characters in the stories of Mary, Steve, Helen, and Bob and Ann?

Part 3
Moral Concerns

When death is imminent, a number of moral decisions must be made. Patients must choose among various medical options. Families may be required to make crucial choices for a family member no longer able to do so. Friends and pastors will need to discern the difference between welcomed support and unwanted interference, showing caring concern through calls and visits while still respecting the dying person's physical limitations and need for privacy. Health care professionals must balance their obligations to patients with society's expectations and their own personal values. It should also be acknowledged that resisting these decisions is simply choosing not to decide.

Moral reflection and discernment must take into account the circumstances that force these decisions, as well as the most deeply held beliefs, values, and commitments that shape our perceptions and responses. So far, we have surveyed the contemporary landscape of dying and death and examined some theological themes that shape our moral vision and conduct as Christians. The final task is to see how our present circumstances and theological vocabulary might inform our moral reflection and discernment. Once again, the intent of this part is not to prescribe a particular course of action but to invite the reader to think and ponder.

Recent developments in medicine force us to engage in a crucial debate, literally one of life-and-death proportions. We are being urged to redefine what a good life and death now mean. We are besieged with such facile questions as: Is there a right to die? Is there a right to live? Is there a moral obligation not to live too long? As citizens we have already entered this debate. It is also of paramount importance, however, that the church lend its voice in shaping public policies. Yet more important, we must determine if these are the questions we are called, as Christians, to ask, let alone answer, when it comes to fashioning a good and faithful life and death.

Chapter 4 in this part describes various approaches to moral reflection and discernment. Chapter 5 examines some moral questions raised by dying and death.

4

Approaches to Moral Reflection and Discernment

Ethics is often popularly perceived as a gray area, confusing and highly subjective. Every moral issue produces a seemingly endless stream of conflicting commentary, analysis, and solutions, never achieving a consensus about what is right or wrong. The current state of ethical discourse has been characterized as "moral cheerleading" leading to interminable debate.[1] For many people, ethics is confined to the opinion page of the newspaper where columnists challenge or confirm the prejudices of the reader.

One reason for this disparate collection of ethical judgments on almost any issue is a lack of agreement on how moral reflection and discernment can best be pursued. As Keith Berndtson has written:

> Where should an ethical inquiry begin? Most analyses are informed by theory, and most theories of ethics can be boiled down to their first questions. Aristotle, for example, began with the questions "What is my purpose?" and "What is good?" Kant began with the questions "What is my duty?" and "What is right?"[2]

Consequently, moral disagreement may result because the disputants are asking dissimilar questions. They literally talk past rather than with each other while describing a moral problem and proposing a solution. It is somewhat like two persons trying to have a conversation but speaking two different languages. Out of frustration they may start yelling at each other, mistakenly believing the increased volume will somehow improve communication and resolve the dilemma.

Furthermore, individuals may be asking the same questions, and share a common moral language, yet disagree over what the terms mean and how they should be applied. For example, there may be a shared commitment that the primary ethical questions require reflecting on and discerning one's purpose or duty. Yet there may be honest disputes regarding what one's purpose or duty means at the end of life.

The relatively recent development of "bioethics" or "biomedical ethics" as a specialized form of moral inquiry reflects these larger problems accompanying moral philosophy and theology. Bioethicists using differing moral theories will often offer conflicting accounts of dying and death. Or some bioethicists may share a common moral theory but disagree over the ethics of euthanasia or physician-assisted suicide.

In addition, although bioethics has helped identify and clarify the moral decisions that must be made at the end of life, its relevancy for Christian reflection and discernment is limited. When theologians comment on bioethical issues they must usually translate the theological terms they use into a secular vocabulary to demonstrate their practical and public pertinence. Many theologians have eagerly embraced this task, but the work that results is often only mildly religious rather than overtly Christian, failing to inform the church's mission and ministry to the dying.[3]

To help clarify some of the ethical concerns associated with dying and death the following sections will briefly describe prevalent approaches to moral reflection and discernment. The first two sections are overviews of two traditionally dominant and contending ethical theories. The next two sections summarize critiques of these traditional theories and present alternative approaches to moral reflection and discernment. The last two sections elaborate the sanctity of life and quality of life positions introduced in chapter 1.

Deontological Ethics

Deontological ethics is one traditional strand or resource for constructing moral theories. Deontological theories stress the central role of imperative duties; the term comes from the Greek words *deon*, meaning "duty," and *logos*, meaning "science." Moral duties are not imaginative inventions but are derived from fundamental laws of nature or divine commands. Many deontological theories "hold that duties are self-evident in much the same way that the elementary truths of arithmetic are self-evident."[4] In addition, moral duties are universal because they remain true regardless of one's history, culture, or personal experience. In making moral decisions a person is, therefore, obligated to fulfill a duty regardless of the consequences for the one making and those affected by the decision. A moral act is judged to be right in and of itself, never in comparison with the results or repercussions. When applied to theology, deontological theories construe Christian ethics as obedience to divine commands revealed in scripture or in the doctrines and teachings of the church.

To determine whether particular deeds are right or wrong a deontological theory of ethics must give a reasoned account of universal principles that inform one's moral reasoning. Many of these theories start with a supreme or overarching moral principle or command. Kant's "categorical imperative," for example, argued that we should do only what can be universally willed, or as more popularly portrayed, that people should be treated only as an end and never as a means.

Secondary principles are derived from supreme or overarching commands. Such principles as "Do not lie" or "Do not steal" follow from Kant's categorical imperative. These secondary principles establish a hierarchy of duties, obligations, and rules of conduct. I am, for example, obligated to tell you the truth, or I have a duty to protect your property from thieves. A priority of duties is needed to resolve those situations when they come into conflict. As Ruth Macklin has written: "If a person is simultaneously confronted with two possible actions—saving a life and keeping a dinner engagement—the action of saving a life is the higher duty. Of course, not all choices between conflicting duties are as obvious as this one."[5]

Within deontological ethical theories, immoral or unethical conduct may result from either willfully disregarding or neglecting to perform one's duty. For example, it is wrong if I tell you a lie or do nothing to prevent your property from being stolen. It must be stressed, however, that this judgment is not based on the consequences of my action or inaction. Telling you a lie is not wrong because it may hurt your feelings or deceive you, nor is failing to protect your property wrong because you suffer a loss. These acts are wrong because I have failed to carry out moral duties that should be universally willed. It is reasonable to want everyone to tell the truth or respect the property of others. It is not reasonable, however, to want everyone to lie or steal.

Deontological ethical theories have exerted a strong influence in the development of bioethics. Bioethicists have proposed supreme or overarching principles defining the practice of medicine as a universal good. It is reasonable, for instance, to will that every person should live a long and healthy life. Secondary principles are then derived regarding the moral practice of medicine.[6] Tom L. Beauchamp and James F. Childress, for example, argue that these principles include autonomy, "where the individual determines his or her own fate";[7] nonmaleficence, "where no harm or injury are to be knowingly inflicted upon a patient";[8] beneficence, where we have "the duty to help others further their important and legitimate interests";[9] and justice, understood "in terms of fairness," where a "person has been given what he is due or owed."[10] When applied to specific medical cases these principles should be violated only under extremely rare or unique situations. Specific duties, codes, and rules, therefore, are formulated which govern the actions of health care professionals and their relationships with patients. Surgeons, for instance, are prohibited from performing surgeries without the informed consent of autonomous patients, or their guardians or surrogates.

The primary disputes among deontological bioethicists involve the formulation and priority of principles, as well as their practical application. There is, for instance, no universal consensus regarding what constitutes a good and long life. How can it be objectively or universally determined when a person has lived a life that is good enough or long enough? Formulating and applying secondary principles are also subject to severe disagreements. How is the autonomy of children and incompetent patients best honored? Should a just distribution of medical resources be based on need or merit? Furthermore, how are conflicts between different principles best resolved? For instance, what should be done if a patient requests a surgical procedure (the principle of autonomy) that a physician believes is likely to subject him or her to unwarranted risk or potential harm (the principle of nonmaleficence)?

In addition to disputes among philosophers, theologians, and bioethicists influenced by the deontological tradition, there is also a competing source of ethical theories that is critical of its purpose and methods. It is toward this other traditional approach to moral reflection and discernment that we now turn our attention.

Teleological Ethics

Teleological, or consequentialist, ethics is the other dominant traditional strand or resource for constructing moral theory. Within a teleological framework acts are judged to be good or bad in light of their purposes, goals, ends, results, or consequences. Duties have no intrinsic value, and morality is not "an end in itself, but . . . a means to something else."[11] Unlike that of deontological ethics, the moral task of teleological ethics is not to discover what is universally true or right and then act accordingly but to thoughtfully choose a course of action which best achieves a desirable future. As Macklin summarizes:

> Consequentialism has several variations, but its central meaning is captured by an imperative: "Choose the action most likely to bring about the best results." Since human actions often have mixed consequences—unwanted results as well as desired ones—the consequentialist principle is sometimes cast as the formula "Choose the action likely to result in a balance of benefits over harms."[12]

The goals or ends that should be achieved, however, are not arbitrary or subject to personal whim. Teleological theories are also shaped by reasoned principles providing standards for judging between good and bad options. Utilitarianism and pragmatism, for instance, are teleological forms of moral reasoning. Utilitarian or pragmatic principles are used to identify the difference between potential good or bad consequences of specific acts.

Jeremy Bentham, an early utilitarian, argued that morality should help increase pleasure and avoid pain. A later utilitarian, John Stuart Mill, proposed a more elaborate scheme, claiming that "morality should be empirically based, ascertaining first what people really find 'desirable' and then arranging society so that as much as possible (quantitatively as well as qualitatively) of what people desire can be obtained, by as many as possible, in an orderly and co-operative way."[13] When teleological theories are applied to selected theological themes, Christian ethics becomes a process of discerning which acts are most compatible with divine promises regarding the Kingdom of God or a new creation.

Within teleological ethics whether one should tell a lie or the truth depends on the situation and the anticipated consequences. I may justify lying to you, for example, because it increases the overall pleasure of the individuals involved in a particular situation. Or, even though there may be some general agreement that stealing is undesirable and therefore bad, whether or not I will protect your property from thieves is subject to various considerations. On the one hand I may try to prevent the theft of your property, believing I will be successful or that I may set an example inspiring greater vigilance in the future, thereby increasing the overall pleasure of society. On the other hand I may conclude that the risks far outweigh any benefits, and my unsuccessful effort, injury, or death will only increase the undesirable effects of the theft.

What must be emphasized is that, from the perspective of teleological ethics, telling the truth, lying, stealing, protecting or failing to protect property have nothing to do with accomplishing, or failing to accomplish, moral duties. An act or decision is judged to be good or bad not because of any intrinsic qualities but solely on its consequences. Although it may be presumed that it is usually desirable to tell the truth or respect the property of others, this may not always prove to be the case. Particular historical, social, and personal circumstances are not irrelevant considerations as they are in deontological ethics but may be important dimensions of moral reflection and discernment.

Teleological ethical theories have also influenced the development of bioethics. Teleologically oriented bioethicists often begin with a premise that some general principle regarding pleasure, happiness, or other desirable goal should govern the practice of medicine. These general principles provide a basis for moral judgment because they reveal "certain experiences and conditions in life that are good in themselves without reference to their further consequences, and that all values are ultimately to be gauged in terms of these intrinsic goods. Health and freedom from pain would be included among such values by most utilitarians."[14]

Since general principles reflect intrinsic values or goods, secondary principles concerning autonomy, nonmaleficence, beneficence, and justice are then derived, providing a basis for the norms of medical practice. Unlike deontological theories, however, these principles and rules do not indicate universal duties that everyone is expected to fulfill and honor. They are, rather, guidelines assisting a process of moral reflection and discernment. Particular goals, objectives, risks, and potential benefits, as well as physical, social, and personal considerations, must be assessed before a moral decision regarding a course of treatment is made.

There is, among teleologically oriented bioethicists, sharp disagreement regarding which general principles should be used, the priority of secondary principles, and their applicability to medical practice. There is no consensus, for instance, that maximizing pleasure, assisting good health, or working toward some other desirable goal provides the best general principle for medical care. In addition, there is no clear priority of secondary principles, or agreement on whether they should remain constant or shift in rank with each particular situation. For example, it may be argued that the overall happiness or pleasure of society would be increased if medical resources were allocated primarily to patients with a high likelihood for full recovery rather than to patients with chronic or terminal conditions. In such a situation, how would a physician best reconcile the principle of justice (allocating medical resources) with the principle of nonmaleficence (not injuring chronic or terminal patients)? Or suppose a doctor is treating two patients who have the same serious and potentially life-threatening illness. In addition, their psychological state is crucial in the treatment of their illness. The doctor believes that one patient is courageous and that knowing the truth about her condition will help her fight the disease, while the other is cowardly and prone to depression that might prove fatal. In these situations, how should the principles of autonomy and beneficence best be reconciled? Which purposes, goals, objectives, and consequences would justify the decisions?

Along with deontological models teleological theories have exerted a deep and profound influence on ethics in general and bioethics in particular. These necessarily brief and highly generalized accounts do not do justice to their complex and articulate arguments, nor have the most significant critiques of each other's arguments and methods been reviewed.[15]

It should also not be assumed that deontological and teleological theories have been unchallenged in the development of ethical theory and bioethics. Some critiques of these traditionally dominant theories, as well as alternative approaches to moral reflection and discernment, are described in the following two sections.

Narrative Ethics

A narrative approach to moral reflection and discernment grows out of criticism of the ethical frameworks shaped by deontological and teleological theories. These traditional ethical frameworks, it is argued, seek theoretical consistency at the expense of truthful descriptions of actual moral conduct, focusing attention on ethical dilemmas rather than on the moral character of persons. One result is elaborate ethical theories that remain abstract and artificial when applied to practical circumstances, producing an unrealistic, ad hoc approach to moral reflection and discernment.

In pursuit of theoretical consistency, philosophers and ethicists spend a great deal of time arguing for or against different moral principles. Yet, with little consensus regarding the primacy or priority of principles, or casually mixing principles from these theoretical systems, the resulting ethical acts "cannot be trusted to yield morally acceptable decisions or judgments."[16] Ironically, theoretical consistency often leads to practical disparities, because "two persons using these principles correctly can reach very different conclusions—one going the utilitarian route, and the other, the deontological."[17] In addition, when applying moral principles to practical circumstances, the procedure is abstract and artificial, missing the rich and complex fabric of actual deliberation as well as the character of the persons involved. In short, theoretically consistent reasoning is not necessarily synonymous with good moral acts. Indeed, it "obligates us to regard our life as an observer would."[18] The primary task of ethics is not to solve problems or dilemmas but to describe or give an account of how a good life should be lived.

Furthermore, a presumption that ethics is based on universal principles destroys the fabric of moral and religious communities based on particular beliefs, convictions, stories, and practices. Insisting on theoretical consistency and universality strips these communities of their morally evocative and formative power. Stanley Hauerwas has observed: "Christian social ethics too often takes the form of principles and policies that are not clearly based on or warranted by the central convictions of the faith."[19]

Other critics argue that traditional ethical theories have used exclusively masculine approaches to moral reasoning but present them as universally valid and normative. Feminist approaches to moral reflection and discernment are largely ignored or discounted. Traditional ethical theories portray a narrow and restricted account of moral perception and experience. There is growing evidence, for instance, that women value relationships over autonomy and perceive justice in relational terms rather than as a process for resolving conflicting claims.[20] What pose as universal ethical theories and principles may in fact be nothing more than disguised patriarchal modes of thought and action, thus impoverishing our moral life.

A narrative approach to ethics asserts that moral vision and conduct are embedded in a storylike structure of life. Exemplary stories or accounts of a tradition's central beliefs, convictions, virtues, and practices are preserved, reenacted, and passed on within particular religious or moral communities. It is these stories in turn which shape or mold the character of persons within a community. Drawing on Aristotle,[21] the primary ethical question is not "What should I do?" but "What type of person should I become?" or "What type of community should we be?" Consequently, a narrative approach to ethics is also often identified as "virtue ethics" or an "ethics of character."

The reason why stories are crucial for the moral life is that they form a historical and eschatological pattern that shapes or defines ethical conduct. A narrative account "attempts to interpret the past and to explain what is done in the present and expected in the future in light of the claims made about the past."[22] Hauerwas explains it this way:

> Stories, then, help us ... to relate to our world and our destiny: the origins and goals of our lives, as they embody in narrative form specific ways of acting out that relatedness. So in allowing ourselves to adopt and be adopted by a particular story, we are in fact assuming a set of practices which will shape the ways we relate to our world and destiny.[23]

Morality is the practical enactment of a truthful memory and faithful expectation. As Christians our memory and expectation, and consequently our moral acts, are shaped by the stories of Israel, Jesus, and the church.[24] When we face a moral decision, the most pressing question is not "What is my duty?" or "What end should I achieve?" but rather "What is happening?" and "What is the fitting response to what is happening?"[25] Our moral perceptions and fitting responses are shaped by the stories and traditions that have formed our vision and character. A moral decision is not the culmination of a deliberative process where a consistent deontologically or teleologically inspired principle is then applied, but is a virtuous response resulting from the kind of people we are or have become.

Narrative or virtue ethics has also influenced the development of bioethics, especially in regard to the moral identity of physicians and their relationships with patients. Bioethical literature acknowledges that we "must make judgments of moral value about persons, traits of character, dispositions, motives, and intentions."[26] With these concerns in mind, a "virtue model of the physician-patient relationship would ask what sort of character an ideal physician ought to have, and what virtues or excellences go to make up that character."[27] Medical school curricula increasingly offer "medicine and literature" courses designed to complement and supplement ethics instruction stressing more traditional approaches.[28] In addition, more elaborate schemes involving a normative understanding of medicine as a moral practice and community have also been proposed.[29]

There are, however, a number of unresolved problems regarding the adequacy of narrative or virtue ethics. For instance, how does one judge the veracity of a particular story or narrative account? If the moral vision of a person is embedded in a particular story or tradition, how can a larger or more objective perspective be gained to judge the truthfulness or adequacy of a specific account? Furthermore, how can the often conflicting moral claims of different traditions and communities be resolved or reconciled? Although stories or narrative accounts may assist in developing the character of health care professionals, it is difficult to see how a narrative approach can adequately guide the formulation of medical policies. In a diverse and secular society the task of bioethics, as H. Tristram Engelhardt Jr. has observed, "is not the attempt to live within, or appreciate the implications of, a particular view of the good life and the canons of moral probity. It is rather a solution to the problem of common action by individuals drawn from diverse moral communities and competing views of the good life."[30] It remains unclear whether a narrative approach to medicine is any less arbitrary than what is inspired by deontological or teleological theories. In the absence of theoretical principles, for example, how should a physician relate to patients in a consistent or coherent manner?

Although narrative ethics offers an intriguing alternative to the traditional deontological and teleological approaches, there is another critical response that also needs to be examined.

Moral Casuistry

Casuistry is not an ethical theory but a method of moral reflection and discernment designed to focus attention on particular situations. Its purpose is not to discover or construct universal moral principles but to pursue a deliberative process leading to practical wisdom. Casuistry does not begin with such questions as "What is my duty?" or "What end should be achieved?" but rather tries to identify "similarities and differences between particular types of cases on a practical level."[31] By identifying similarities and differences we may perceive duties or ends that are "wholly consistent with our moral practice."[32] Casuistry, then, is similar, but not identical, to examining "case studies" and "moral taxonomies."

A casuistic approach shares some of the prominent features of narrative ethics in that its objective is to give a moral account and application that is fitting in particular circumstances. Casuistry is conducted within frameworks of specific intellectual, religious, and moral traditions. Yet as a formal method of reflection and discernment, it is not tied to any prior or particular narrative account. As a result it not only assists moral reasoning within a tradition but can also help bypass or resolve ethical stalemates that occur when the principles being considered have no common standard of comparison. A diverse society of conflicting stories or principles can construct common policies and rules of conduct because they are able to reach consensus on what should be done in practical situations while not agreeing on the reasons for these actions. This is accomplished by focusing attention away from what are thought to be universal, abstract, and timeless concerns toward what Stephen Toulmin describes as "particular, local, and timely"[33] considerations. Casuistry is more concerned about what should be done than why it is done.

Although casuistry has an infamous heritage—Pascal, for instance, described it as "an invitation to excuse the inexcusable"[34]—some philosophers and ethicists argue that it needs to be revitalized. What should be avoided is its abuse, for a "properly conceived ... casuistry redresses the excessive emphasis placed on universal rules and invariant principles by moral philosophers and political preachers alike."[35] More important, given the diverse moral circumstances and interests of the contemporary world, a renewed casuistic method is needed. Albert Jonsen and Stephen Toulmin have observed: "In the last few years, discussions of specific circumstances and cases have at last returned to favor. This has happened almost inadvertently as a by-product of the current preoccupation with professional ethics, notably medical ethics."[36] If renewed interest in practical wisdom is to be applied "to new and more complex sets of circumstances, in ways that respect ... human needs,"[37] then an appropriate form of casuistry also needs to be developed.

Casuistry holds some promise for formulating ethical policies, rules, and guidelines governing health care in general, and the care of the dying in particular, in a diverse society. Jonsen and

Toulmin, for instance, worked with the National Commission for the Protection of Human Subjects of Biomedical and Behavioral Research. Its purpose was to examine a wide range of bioethical issues and recommend general guidelines regarding medical research. The commission "included men and women; blacks and whites; Catholics, Protestants, Jews, and atheists; medical scientists and behaviorist psychologists; philosophers; lawyers; theologians; and public interest representatives."[38]

Jonsen and Toulmin were impressed by the remarkable consensus achieved by the commission, and believe it resulted from their focus on a casuistical plane: "So long as the debate stayed on the level of particular judgments, the ... commissioners saw things in much the same way. The moment it soared to the level of 'principles,' they went their separate ways."[39] The casuistry employed avoided the interminable moral debate associated with conflicting theoretical principles while not insisting that individuals jettison their own beliefs and commitments. For "when, as a collective the commission agreed about particular practical judgments, the individual commissioners justified their readiness to join in that consensus by appealing to different 'general principles.' "[40]

The commission's experience implies that public policies governing the medical care of the dying can be established that respect personal values and expectations. Greater moral certitude and sensitivity are achieved with a "shared perception of what [is] specifically at stake in particular kinds of human situations"[41] rather than imposing a set of general or theoretical principles. Moral wisdom is attained when ethical inquiry is based on concrete judgments rather than abstract theories.

Although as a method casuistry may assist moral reflection and discernment, particularly in reconciling irresolvable disputes, a number of problems also need to be acknowledged. It is questionable whether stressing method over content will result in "right" or "truthful" decisions. A practical consensus can as easily be achieved for "bad" as well as "good" reasons. It is also unclear how a "properly" conceived casuistry resists the abuse that gave it its well-deserved reputation for excusing the inexcusable. What prevents a search for practical wisdom from degrading into an expedient moral calculus? Furthermore, the method may not be as "neutral" as assumed. It may reflect primarily Western and masculine assumptions on how practical decisions should be made. The fallacy of faith in universal principles may simply be replaced by confidence in a fallacious universal method. Significant questions and perceptions could be arbitrarily ignored by unwittingly excluding feminist and other cultural approaches to moral reflection and discernment. It is also not clear how casuistry would assist the church in providing a ministry to the dying. Ignoring theological beliefs and commitments is not synonymous with suspending ethical principles when a community is attempting to faithfully discern the will and calling of God.

Once again these brief descriptions of narrative ethics and moral casuistry do not capture the rich fabric of their claims and arguments. Yet along with deontological and teleological theories they help to portray the complex and varied landscape of moral reflection and discernment. As reflected in the illustrative concerns presented in chapter 5, differing perceptions lead to very different assessments, judgments, and decisions at the end of life. Before looking at these concerns, however, we must first elaborate two important beliefs that were introduced earlier, for the positions of sanctity of life and quality of life influence each of the approaches described above.

Sanctity of Life

As previously mentioned, a sanctity of life position holds that humans are unique and must be honored and respected under any and all circumstances. There are both religious and secular forms of this belief or claim. A religious perspective may believe that humans are endowed with special characteristics, such as reason or a soul, or are created in the image of God, which bestows upon them an exacting moral status. A human life should be taken only under rare and extraordinary circumstances because the power over life and death rightfully belong to God. We are obligated to preserve and protect human life as part of our sacred trust or duty.

A secular version of this argument does not invoke a deity to bestow value to human life but nonetheless insists that there are normative dimensions of human existence that should be venerated. When human life is casually abused or neglected, we react with an intuitive sense of outrage or sacrilege.[42] There is a "natural metaphysic" which affirms that life is "sacred because it is life."[43] This natural sanctity is reflected in our "elemental sensation" of vitality, lineage, and fear of extinction.[44] No divine force is needed to inspire our profound respect and admiration for human life. Human progress is blunted when the lives of individuals are casually or prematurely terminated.

In its most extreme form a sanctity of life position insists that personal longevity must be extended for as long as possible. Every medical means available should be employed in a fight against death. Consequently, any form of euthanasia, suicide, or medical practice that would hasten death is rejected. A less extreme version opposes active forms of euthanasia and suicide but does not insist that all medical means to prolong life should always be used. A so-called divinely appointed hour of one's death should not be vainly resisted, and terminal illnesses can be allowed to run their course.[45] There is, however, a strong moral presumption that medicine should be used to prolong life rather than hasten death.

A sanctity of life position can influence the ethical theories and approaches described above. A deontological ethic, for instance, may formulate a general principle that "Life is better than death," or a rule that insists "Never kill." A teleological approach may presume that the burden of proof rests on disproving the principle that pleasure or happiness is normally diminished with death. A narrative ethic may insist that only God should choose the time of a person's death, or careful casuistic scrutiny of particular cases may reveal that extending longevity is an overriding consideration in treating the dying.

Religious and secular advocates of a sanctity of life position may also share a belief that contemporary society is sliding into an abyss where human life is debased and devalued. The specter of Walker Percy's *The Thanatos Syndrome*, it is argued, is becoming a reality in which killing and "euthanasia are routine therapies for the physically and mentally impaired, for the 'unwanted' and socially 'useless.' "[46] It is feared that we are simultaneously developing the technological capability and moral insensitivity in which our desire "to rationalize the killing of... suffering people knows no limit."[47] In response a sanctity of life position must be rigorously asserted against the current of our age, for "it provides the only ultimate foundation for the protection by public and professional opinion... against sadism in its more crude and brutal forms."[48] The taking of human life, particularly the lives of persons entrusted to medical care, should not be the province of individual decision or the prerogative of expedient social policies. It is a decision better left to the wisdom of moral communities, or divine providence.

Quality of Life

A quality of life position asserts that the primary goal of caring for the dying should be to help them achieve a death that reflects their values, desires, and wishes. It is the quality rather than the length of one's life that should capture medical attention. What is of paramount importance are "personal choices about one's own life, how it is to be lived, and the extent to which medicine will or will not be utilized in achieving one's own goals."[49]

Once again, there are both religious and secular dimensions to this position. From a religious perspective it is argued that physical existence is not of ultimate value. Spiritual and relational considerations come into account when treating a dying patient. A point may be reached when the qualities of these spiritual and relational considerations are so greatly diminished that continued existence becomes an unwarranted and unwanted burden. In the face of prolonged suffering or a persistent vegetative state, for instance, ending a life is an act of mercy. Consequently, euthanasia, and perhaps suicide,[50] mark responsible reactions to terminal illnesses because "life is not a value to be preserved in and for itself."[51]

A more secular position declares that individuals have the right to determine their own fate. It is up to each person to decide whether his or her own life is worth living. If it is decided that a life is no longer worth living, then medicine should assist patients in setting the time and means of their own deaths. James Rachels, for example, argues that human life should be understood in terms of biography rather than biology.[52] For Rachels, "having a life" is not synonymous with "merely being alive."[53] We are "complex creatures who have a rich mix of desires and aspirations."[54] We are "curious" and "gregarious"; we "form friendships and seek the company of others."[55] When these qualities are no longer present, an individual may be technically alive but does not have a life. A body performing biological rhythms is not equivalent to a person who has a life. When such a point is reached, then medical, legal, and moral constraints should not be imposed to prevent the ending of a life.

Extreme advocates of this position maintain that there should be few, if any, limitations on when individuals can choose to end their own lives. Since the value of one's life is a personal judgment, severely ill or incompetent patients should be assisted in achieving what they judge to be a desirable death as long as their decisions do not injure or unduly burden others. A less extreme view would limit euthanasia, suicide, and assisted suicide to terminally ill, severely disabled, or comatose persons. There is a strong presumption, however, that health care professionals should honor reasonable requests of dying patients, and that the principal goal of caring for the dying should be to provide comfort rather than extend life.

A quality of life position can also influence the ethical theories and approaches described previously. A deontological ethic may emphasize the principle of "autonomy" and the accompanying rule of the patient's "right to choose." A teleological approach may argue that pleasure or happiness is increased when individuals are assisted in achieving a death they find desirable. A narrative ethic can insist that assisting death is an act of mercy in the face of prolonged suffering. Or casuistic scrutiny of various cases may conclude that both patients and physicians are better served by stressing qualitative rather than clinical considerations.

Quality of life advocates do not believe that the specter of Percy's *Thanatos Syndrome* is the principal moral dilemma facing the dying. The problem, rather, is the technological imperative that has gripped medicine. In the name of extending life, too often medicine simply delays death and prolongs suffering. In order for patients to protect themselves from unwanted and undesirable medical procedures, they should have the ability to control the time and means of their own deaths. The Hastings Center concluded: "By allowing patients and their surrogates to make choices that consider 'quality of life,' we diminish the risk of forcing lives of pain, indignity, or overwhelming burden on those who are helpless. By applying the patient's view of quality of life' we also avoid denigrating the worth of individual human beings, and instead respect their values and beliefs."[56]

Again, these brief summaries of the sanctity of life and quality of life positions do not explore the subtle and complex nature of their respective claims and arguments.[57] Yet these two positions exert a strong influence on bioethics. What now remains is to examine how the various ethical theories, approaches, methods, and positions shape the moral decisions that are made by patients, families, friends, and health care professionals at the end of life. These concerns will be explored in chapter 5.

5
Moral Questions Raised by Dying and Death

Moral decisions are shaped by a variety of factors. We must take into account the circumstances that force an immediate choice or action. Crucial life-and-death decisions are made when we or someone we love is dying. Our perception and understanding influence our response. We react differently, for example, depending on whether we see medical technologies as valiant efforts to preserve life or futile efforts that delay death. Our moral principles, beliefs, and commitments inform the decisions we make. Pursuing a good death, for instance, prompts differing actions depending on whether we believe that the value of life is based on its sanctity or its quality.

The purpose of this chapter is modest and limited. The concerns examined illustrate but do not exhaust the wide range of moral questions raised by dying and death. Nor are they elaborate case studies requiring the reader to assume a role and determine what should be done. No attempt is made to examine each concern from every possible angle and then describe how differing ethical theories and approaches might influence conflicting analyses and decisions. Rather, a few general circumstances are described briefly, a perspective or two are interjected, and an ethical theory or approach is mentioned in order to sketch the rough contours of moral reflection and discernment in the face of dying and death. The intent of this chapter, in short, is to encourage introspection and discussion.

Withholding Medical Treatment

When, if ever, should medical treatment be withheld from a dying person? A dying person may reach a point where a crucial decision must be made. Let us say an experimental procedure is available that will not cure the illness but may prolong life for a number of weeks, perhaps months. The side effects, however, will include severe discomfort, restricted mobility, and eventually greater pain or lengthening periods of unconsciousness because of increased dosages of medication. Should the treatment be used or withheld?

For the dying person there are many considerations. Which of my values, beliefs, and convictions are most at stake in this decision? What are my greatest fears, hopes, and expectations? What is my capacity to endure hardship? Do I trust and have confidence in the medical staff providing my care? What emotional support can I expect of my friends and family? What do they expect of me? What will be the financial costs and burdens of my decision? If I submit to this procedure, will the knowledge gained benefit patients in the future? If so, am I willing to make the sacrifice? What is God calling me to do and to be in this decision?

Larger moral beliefs, convictions, or principles, although often not formally invoked, also exert an influence. The dying person may be struggling to determine whether an early death relatively free from pain would be preferable to a longer but more painful life. A physician offers this option out of a sense of duty to the patient, but worries that the effort may prove futile. A spouse may plead to refuse the procedure to spare the loved one future suffering, while a friend urges a fight against death for as long as possible.

Moral complexity is heightened when decisions must be made for others. If a dying patient is incompetent, which treatments should be used and which, if any, withheld? Here the issue is probably not an experimental procedure that may prolong life, but more routine methods that a competent patient could accept or decline. Should the pneumonia of a comatose patient with lung cancer be treated? Should the arrested heart of a person with advanced Alzheimer's disease be resuscitated? Should painful reconstructive surgery be performed on a profoundly retarded child with a congenital heart condition? What is God's will or intention in these circumstances? How can we best discern it?

Furthermore, who should make these decisions? Physicians? An ethics committee? The court? A friend or relative? What decisions would we make, or prefer to be made, if the incompetent dying person were a close friend or sibling? My spouse or my child?

Simply "knowing" what the desires of a person were before an illness or accident rendered him or her incompetent, or trying to put ourselves in the patient's place does not ease the uncertainty of deciding. What if previous instructions were vague? What sense should we make of such general phrases as "I don't want to be a vegetable," or "Keep those tubes out of me." Or what if there are reasons to believe that a person has changed his or her mind? Suppose, for instance, that a person who often railed against "useless" medical procedures eagerly embraced every treatment offered with the onset of a severe illness before slipping into a coma. What is now desired? Or, suppose that identifying with the incompetent dying person is unlikely to lead to a decision that seems reasonable and rational. We quite often make reasoned decisions that others find unreasonable or irrational. In making decisions for others, whose reason and rationality should be used?

Nor do more general principles or beliefs necessarily make the right choice easier. Believing that life is sacred, for example, does not automatically authorize a carte blanche to do everything possible, particularly if there is a providential dimension to a timely death. A sanctity of life position does not justify mindlessly preserving a collection of biological organs. Nor should a quality of life orientation require that all life-prolonging procedures be withheld from an incompetent dying person. We really do not know if the quality of life for the incompetent dying person has reached a point where death is desired, nor should the quality standards of the "healthy" be arbitrarily imposed upon the "ill." The merciful impulse that values a quality of life can, without great care and vigilance, become disfigured into a heartless form of quality control.

When, if ever, should medical treatment be withheld from a dying person?

Euthanasia

When, if ever, should we allow a person to die or hasten death?

The moral questions accompanying euthanasia, particularly in its passive, voluntary, and nonvoluntary forms, are similar to those raised by withholding treatment. Here the focus is on circumstances and perspectives that lead to conflicting values, as well as on the question whether we are moving toward an implicitly more active and involuntary practice of euthanasia.

Ideally, opting for euthanasia reflects a rigorous process of personal reflection. An individual has thoughtfully determined what types of medical procedures should or should not be used in treating a terminal disease. Detailed instructions regarding treatment are written in what is called an "advance directive" which the person expects will be followed should an illness or accident render him or her incompetent. The individual discusses the directive with his or her physician and a person who has agreed to act as a surrogate should incompetency occur. In addition, formal procedures for drafting and filing the advance directive are followed to ensure that the individual's wishes are legal, fully informed, and noncoerced.

If all parties believe that an individual has the right to exert such control, there is little quarrel with this ideal arrangement. It is this belief, however, that creates much of the conflict between moral principles and claims. For example, it is difficult to imagine how sanctity of life and quality of life positions, as well as deontological claims stressing a duty to live and teleological claims stressing pleasure, could be reconciled in a common set of legal policies and ethical constraints governing the practice of euthanasia. Seemingly one perspective would need to be imposed at the expense of the other, creating in turn additional moral problems or concerns. "Conservative" euthanasia policies, for instance, could increase suicides by individuals who fear an "undignified" death or would prompt a new wave of "mercy killing" by anguished friends or relatives. "Liberal" euthanasia policies could create a public perception of distrust and fear that dying patients will be abandoned or urged not to live "too long" because the law and ethical codes permit the choice of an "early exit."

The moral dilemma becomes even more complex when active euthanasia is permitted.[1] A competent dying person experiencing a profoundly diminished quality of life could request active euthanasia. Following an extensive review of the request to determine that it is fully informed and freely chosen, a health care professional would be permitted to prepare and administer a lethal injection or some other medical procedure to bring about a quick and painless death.

Such a proposal not only rehearses once again the moral debates described above but also introduces new concerns regarding the proper role of medicine. Should health care professionals, even when motivated by mercy, ever become agents of death? Is the taking of life so antithetical to the work of healing that attempting to combine these roles would result in public confusion and distrust? Furthermore, how would such principles as autonomy and beneficence best be reconciled and consistently applied in a situation where some dying patients actively seek death while others fight against it for as long as possible? Will health care professionals simply be expected to acquiesce to any request or demand? In addition, to Christians, is active euthanasia compatible with a belief that our lives are not our own but belong to God?[2]

It should not be assumed that the "ideal" situation of clearly articulated advance directives is the norm. Many dying or chronically ill patients become incompetent without ever having expressed their desires or expectations for future care. What should be done in these circumstances?

The contemporary "death with dignity" or "right to die" movement was started largely in reaction to the practice of always using life-prolonging treatments. If an individual's desires were unknown, or even contrary to his or her wishes, life-prolonging procedures were routinely imposed. The practical results, critics charged, were prolonged suffering, escalating costs, and an undignified death. Hence the need for patients to exert greater control over their own medical care, particularly at the end of life.

With growing public acceptance of euthanasia, however, there may now be an implicit presumption that life-prolonging treatments should be withheld rather than employed. If the desires of an incompetent dying person are unknown, or at times contrary to his or her wishes, life-prolonging treatments may be withheld that a physician judges to be pointless, futile, or wasteful.[3] A presumption in favor of euthanasia can simultaneously provide a peaceful death for individuals and contain medical costs.

These changing circumstances, however, also create a number of troubling moral questions. Will a subtle preference to practice euthanasia when the dying person's wishes are unknown damage the relationship of trust between health care professionals and patients? As physicians attempt to balance their duties to their patients with social and political expectations to contain costs, could euthanasia be easily and expediently abused? Will a double standard of care for the dying emerge between those with and without advance directives; between those with and without articulate surrogates; between those with and without an ability to pay for life-prolonging treatments?

It is ironic that recent changes in medical policies reflecting the initiatives of the "death with dignity" or "right to die" movement are now beginning to act as barriers to life-prolonging treatments. Increasingly, will a case need to be made that life-prolonging treatments should be used rather than withheld from a dying and incompetent person whose wishes are unknown? If a quality of life position becomes "normative" for the care of dying patients, how will the rights of those holding a sanctity of life position best be reconciled and protected? In other words, if the moral debates over euthanasia when a "Preserve life at all costs" assumption was in force proved disquieting, the moral debates over euthanasia in a "Let us not needlessly prolong life" environment will prove at least equally troubling. Furthermore, although satisfying ethical solutions might be developed within particular narrative traditions providing a balance between unduly prolonging life or hastening death, should such a scheme be imposed upon a diverse society, or should it be binding only upon those within a particular religious community and tradition?

When, if ever, should we allow a person to die or hasten death?

Physician-assisted Suicide

When, if ever, should a health care professional help a person take his or her own life?

The actions of Dr. Jack Kevorkian have captured a great deal of media, as well as legal, attention. Our reactions may be mixed. We may feel some empathy with his patients. Years of pain and suffering, or the prospect of losing self-control as an illness grows worse, prompt a desperate search for release from the anguish or fear. Yet there is also something troubling and disquieting about a physician who helps individuals end their own lives. We may feel some repulsion when a doctor aids death rather than life. Regardless of our initial reactions, however, physician-assisted suicide forces us to ponder the proper role of medicine in relation to dying and death.

Physician-assisted suicide is not synonymous with either withholding treatment or euthanasia. Withholding treatment allows a patient to die. Passive euthanasia hastens death, and through active euthanasia a health care professional kills a dying patient for presumably humane and compassionate reasons. In physician-assisted suicide, the doctor neither allows, hastens, nor directly causes the death of a patient, but provides the means for a person to end his or her own life.

As might be expected, there is no consensus regarding the morality of physician-assisted suicide. On the one hand, if one does not have any moral qualms regarding withholding treatment or voluntary passive or active euthanasia, physician-assisted suicide is one more option which may be used to achieve a desirable death. A doctor is merely helping a patient control the time and means of death in a quick and painless manner. Quality of life arguments, teleological claims, and deontological principles stressing autonomy can all be invoked to justify physician-assisted suicide. On the other hand, if one believes that withholding treatment or euthanasia is wrong, then physician-assisted suicide is also an immoral act. If a doctor should not hasten or cause death, then neither should an attempt to end one's own life be assisted. Sanctity of life arguments, teleological claims, and deontological principles stressing duty can also be appealed to in objecting to physician-assisted suicide.

Moral reflection and discernment become more complex when the intent, rather than the act, commands our attention. Withholding medical treatment or passive euthanasia may, for a variety of reasons, be permissible, since the intent is not to kill the patient. For example, although withholding antibiotics or increasing dosages of morphine may hasten death, the purpose is not to end life but to spare the dying patient unnecessary discomfort or pain. Death in these circumstances is foreseen but not intended, and health care professionals neither directly cause nor assist the taking of a life. A patient can be allowed to die or death may be indirectly hastened, but a dying person should never be directly killed through active euthanasia or assisted in committing suicide.

Some philosophers, theologians, and ethicists argue, however, that there is no qualitative difference between allowing a person to die, assisting a suicide, or killing a competent patient who makes such a request. The intent is irrelevant, and attending to this artificial distinction is hypocritical since the result is the same in any case. Whether a health care professional does nothing to prevent death or assists a dying person to commit suicide is not the issue at stake. What is of paramount importance is that a dying person be provided the care that he or she desires in a humane and merciful manner. In some cases this may best be accomplished by assisting a dying person to take his or her own life.

As might be expected, the ethical theories and approaches described in chapter 4 do not easily settle this dispute. Deontological principles can be invoked on both sides—a duty to live verses the autonomous right of patients to make their own choices. Teleological arguments can be mustered that society is best served if health care professionals do not kill or assist the death of their patients, but it can also be argued that there is greater social benefit when individuals are free, and at times helped, to determine their own fate. One narrative tradition may proclaim that life is never ours to take, while another community may insist that suicide marks an honorable and dignified death.

The principal moral questions raised up to this point assume that the person seeking physician-assisted suicide is dying. Does the situation change if a person is not dying but is severely incapacitated? Suppose, for example, that an active young adult is injured in a sporting accident. The person now suffers severe paralysis that greatly restricts physical mobility. A once energetic and independent individual is now confined to a wheelchair or bed, and nearly constant care must be provided by family, friends, or health care professionals.

Persons in these circumstances are not dying and can live to an old age, but they may also come to believe that the quality of their lives is so greatly diminished that they would be better off dead. In such a situation should a physician assist a suicide if requested by a competent adult? If one believes that medicine should never directly cause or assist the death of a dying person, then clearly it would be an even greater evil to help end the life of one who is disabled but not dying. If one believes, however, that suicide is a matter of individual choice or right, a physician may legitimately help persons who are physically unable to take their own lives.

The moral problem becomes more complex when considered in the context of providing medical care and the conduct expected of health care professionals. It is one thing to consider allowing, hastening, assisting, or causing the death of a dying person. As we have seen, each of these options can elicit moral, albeit controversial, support. What do these options entail, however, for a person who is severely disabled but not dying? For example, what type of medical treatment should be withheld to allow or hasten death? If the cardiac, respiratory, and digestive systems are functioning, should food and water be withheld? Furthermore, if a disabled person refuses to eat, should medical personnel intervene to keep the person alive against his or her will? Is refusing to take nutrition the same as exercising the right to refuse medical treatment?

How should we respond to severely disabled persons who no longer wish to live but lack the physical strength or mobility to commit suicide? There are a variety of perspectives to consider before attempting any answer. It is not only a situation where a disabled individual has made a decision and requests assistance in accomplishing it. To what extent should the wishes and desires of family and friends and their ability to provide support influence a decision? What bearing should the beliefs of an individual's community of faith and their willingness to provide care have? To what extent should the moral beliefs and values of health care professionals be respected? What impact would physician-assisted suicides have on health care institutions? Would such acts diminish their standing as institutions dedicated to healing? If severely physically disabled persons are assisted by physicians in committing suicide, should requests by severely mentally and emotionally disabled persons also be honored? What are the legitimate interests of society in regulating or prohibiting physician-assisted suicide? How is God's will or intention known in these circumstances? Who is in the best position to discern what should be done?

When, if ever, should a health care professional help a person take his or her own life?

Access to Treatment

When, if ever, should personal factors and characteristics determine our care of the dying?

Containing the cost of health care is a controversial and volatile issue in bioethics. One way to control costs is to limit access to selected medical treatments and procedures. Some countries, for instance, invest very little in so-called high-tech instruments, while other nations restrict or prohibit a number of elective surgeries. A few societies impose criteria regarding age or potential success to determine the type of medical treatment available to a patient. Organ transplants, for example, are not performed past a specified age, or surgery is not authorized if it is unlikely that a desirable recovery will result.

As health care reform is debated in the United States, a desire to contain costs may influence the type of care offered to the dying. Restricting or limiting access to certain types of treatments would reduce costs. Some activists have proposed national policies that would limit care of the dying to controlling pain and providing comfort. Financial resources would be allocated to less expensive hospice and home care rather than expensive hospitalization, high-tech devices, and experimental treatments that merely delay an inevitable death. Such a policy, it is argued, would be both less costly and ultimately more humane. Opponents counter, however, that such a scheme would destroy such traditional values as freedom of choice, autonomy, and a free market. Denying access to a full range of medical options, it is alleged, might benefit the economy (though this is far from certain), but at the expense of victimizing dying persons.

For a number of political, social, and economic reasons it is unlikely that sweeping policy changes will be implemented in the foreseeable future. What is receiving serious attention, however, is the question whether personal factors and characteristics should be considered in determining what type of care is provided.

Should the age of a dying person, for instance, be considered when determining what type of treatment is offered? Suppose there are two individuals suffering from advanced heart disease. Both will soon die unless a heart transplant is performed. One patient is sixty-eight years old; the other is thirty-eight. Should the older patient be denied a heart transplant and the younger patient given one? Some ethicists would answer yes because the older patient has already lived a relatively long life. Extending a life for perhaps a few more years will add little, and this costly procedure and scarce resource could be put to better use in a patient who would benefit more from the treatment in terms of potential longevity and productivity. From this perspective there is a morally significant difference between an older and younger patient which should be taken into account in determining their respective treatments.

Other ethicists argue, however, that age should be an irrelevant consideration. Patients with a similar illness should receive similar treatment regardless of any difference in age because we cannot accurately predict the consequences of a particular act. An older patient receiving a heart transplant may experience years of enriched personal experience as well as making valuable contributions to family and community. A younger patient may experience a diminished quality of life due to a psychological disorder, engage in immoral or criminal behavior, or be killed in an accident shortly after the surgery. Since we do not know the outcome, age should not be *the* determining factor in allocating medical resources. Relative youth is not necessarily synonymous with a superior quality of life, nor is advanced age any barometer of personal happiness or social utility. Furthermore, a deontological understanding of justice is not served through discriminating practices based on age. Determining whether to perform a life-prolonging treatment should be a medical decision rather than a consequence of how long one has already lived.

It has also been proposed that individuals with chronic or

potentially terminal conditions not receive costly life-prolonging treatments. Individuals diagnosed with HIV or carrying the gene for Huntington's disease, for instance, would be disqualified from receiving organ transplants. Such treatments would merely delay an inevitable death and result in a wasteful allocation of medical resources and increased costs for society. In addition, medical intervention under these circumstances may prove unintentionally cruel by offering a false sense of hope to patients. The intent is not to inflict a heartless policy upon unfortunate individuals but an attempt to control costs through a realistic allocation of medical resources in which prior conditions or illnesses are legitimate factors to consider. The limited purpose of medicine is, after all, to restore health or provide comfort, not merely to delay death by doing everything possible.

Many of the same arguments opposing discrimination against patients on the basis of age also apply in the case of prior chronic or potentially terminal conditions. We cannot predict what quality of life or social utility will result following life-prolonging treatment given to those with or without prior chronic or potentially life-threatening conditions. In addition, many ethicists argue that medical judgment, not economics, should drive the treatment of any patient.

A disturbing caveat also needs to be added. Withholding life-prolonging treatments from persons with prior chronic or potentially terminal conditions may set an alarming precedent for future medical care. We are rapidly developing the ability to screen, diagnose, and correct a growing number of genetically related disorders.[4] If parents fail to prevent or correct these disorders in their offspring we may face the prospect of denying life-prolonging treatments to individuals who are judged to be "not worth the effort" because of the potentially chronic or terminal traits they carry. Those judged to be genetically or biologically "fit" would receive the "best" medical care because of the greater "return" on the "investment" of medical resources. Perhaps unwittingly, a foundation could be laid for an implicit eugenics program[5] in which medical care is based more on genetic or biological characteristics than on physical need.

It has also been proposed that persons who develop terminal

illnesses associated with voluntary lifestyles should be denied access to expensive life-prolonging treatments. Care and comfort, rather than costly surgical or high-tech procedures, should be the primary medical response to an inevitable death caused by personal choices. A heavy smoker dying of lung cancer, for instance, should be provided relief from pain but not offered experimental and costly procedures that may extend life for a few weeks. An alcoholic dying of cirrhosis of the liver should not be a candidate for a liver transplant. The intent is not to punish an individual for making what society may judge to be an irresponsible decision, but to provide an incentive to exercise personal responsibility and control costs.

Many chronic and terminal diseases could be prevented if individuals were encouraged to live healthier lifestyles. Access to health care at the end of life based on prior responsible behavior would offer a powerful incentive. Unlike age or genetic traits, lifestyles are the result of personal freedom and will, such as deciding to smoke or drink, and therefore provide a just and potentially effective criterion for determining what type of health care should be provided at the end of life.

It may be objected that discriminating on the basis of lifestyle or personal choice is not as fair or just as advocates assume, nor is such a policy compatible with traditional medical values. Traditionally medicine has treated an illness regardless of the circumstances that produced it. Out of a sense of mercy and compassion, notorious sinners and exemplary saints are equal in the eyes of medicine and receive what is judged to be appropriate treatment. If the goal is to contain costs, then everyone should have the same limited access to medical treatment at the end of life. Although such a policy would mark a sharp break with the traditional practice of medicine, it would at least mark a fair or just distribution of medical resources. Without broader or more universal criteria for denying access to life-prolonging treatments, rationing medical resources based on lifestyle becomes a form of punishing individuals for making what are judged to be irresponsible decisions.

Furthermore, which lifestyles or personal choices supposedly causing a terminal illness would disqualify an individual from receiving costly life-prolonging treatments? For instance, if a person chooses a highly stressful profession and develops heart disease as a result, should he or she be denied expensive bypass surgery or a heart transplant? Are individuals who work with hazardous chemicals exercising poor judgment? Although many sexually transmitted diseases can be easily treated and cured, should antibiotics be withheld because individuals have exhibited a lack of self-control or failed to take proper precautions? If life-prolonging treatments are withheld from persons in response to their lifestyles, it must also be considered at what point medicine, a traditional fount of mercy and compassion, is transformed into an agent of punishment at the end of life.

Finally, it has been suggested that individuals suffering a highly diminished quality of life should not be subjected to futile attempts to delay death when they become seriously or terminally ill. A profoundly retarded child with a congenital heart defect, for example, should not be subjected to a series of expensive and painful surgeries to repair the defective heart. Such a life-prolonging treatment is both wasteful and cruel. The surgical techniques will not result in a quality of life that the vast majority of people would judge to be desirable or even acceptable. Repairing the heart of a profoundly retarded child is merely extending a life of suffering, as well as compounding the misery since the child lacks the intellectual ability to comprehend the reasons for the pain and discomfort inflicted by the surgeries. There is no humane reason why expensive life-prolonging treatments should be expended in a tragic but hopeless situation.

In response it can be objected that these arguments are nothing more than an attempt to impose standards of quality by the healthy and mentally competent upon the sick and mentally incompetent. How can desirable or even minimal levels of quality be determined, particularly for those who cannot express their desires or wishes? It is also not clear whether a profoundly retarded child is suffering or whether we are simply projecting our own fears.[6] If a child with profound mental retardation is not genuinely suffering, why would we hesitate to prolong his or her life by repairing a defective heart? In addition, if we are unwilling to subject such children to the incomprehensible pain of surgery, why are we willing to subject "normal" children to the same procedure even though they may also lack the maturity to fully understand the reasons for their discomfort? A decision to withhold life-prolonging treatments because the "quality" of a life is thought to be so greatly diminished that it need not be continued is to implicitly impose a form of quality control upon the weak and incompetent.

When, if ever, should personal factors and characteristics determine our care of the dying?

Part 3 Summary and Review

The intention of Part 3 was to encourage the reader to reflect on moral decisions that may accompany the end of a life. End-of-life decisions are shaped by a variety of factors involving the circumstances forcing a decision, as well as the beliefs, values, and commitments that form our perspectives, understanding, and eventual responses.

A process of moral reflection and discernment requires organizing this information into a coherent, rational, or satisfying system of thought and action. Chapter 4 reviewed differing approaches to moral inquiry, including deontological and teleological theories, narrative or virtue ethics, casuistry, and sanctity of life and quality of life positions, to help explain why there is much disagreement regarding good or right conduct, particularly when applied to bioethics.

In chapter 5 these differing approaches to moral reflection and discernment were applied to a series of illustrative concerns regarding some selected end-of-life questions. Attention was focused primarily on the often interrelated questions of withholding medical treatment, euthanasia, physician-assisted suicide, and access to treatment.

These chapters have outlined the often baffling array of concerns that accompany dying and death in the contemporary world. There is little consensus regarding how various issues should be resolved, and even little agreement on how the questions should be phrased. Is the principal moral concern, for example, whether modern medicine attempts to prolong life or delay death too long? Do we now have unreasonable expectations regarding our ability to avoid suffering and determine our own fate?

As might be expected, differing answers are offered to the various questions which are asked. The result is often a cacophony of conflicting and contentious voices regarding what should be done. When it comes to dying and death we are a society deeply torn by movements and causes advocating irreconcilable points of view. Such moral urgency and divisiveness should not surprise us, for as Colin E. Gunton has observed, "our age is a matter of extremes." He goes on to add: "Its chief beneficiaries are for the most part better fed, housed, educated, and provided with medical care. The paradox is that in this century the same culture has also consigned more of the many to death by warfare and other modern means of mass destruction."[7]

If larger social, political, and economic extremes are tearing the world apart, a similar pattern holds true when it comes to dying and death. Sanctity of life slogans are met with quality of life mottos. The sentiment to "do everything possible" is matched by a desperate plea to "do as little as needed." Proposals to prohibit euthanasia and physician-assisted suicide are countered by schemes to eliminate any and all restrictions on assisting individuals to end their lives. In reaction to paternalistic medicine, patient autonomy is stressed, often to the exclusion of any other considerations. Compassion and mercy somehow end up being pitted against justice and economic prudence.

As Christians we are not called to become partisans of any particular extreme, or to find some compromise between them. Rather, out of obedience to Christ, we are called to give a truthful account of dying and death, and to be faithfully present to those who are suffering. It is toward providing some rough contours of what our life between the extremes of the present age might mean that we turn our attention in the next and concluding chapter.

Part 3 Discussion Questions

1. Of the various approaches to moral reflection and discernment described in chapter 4, which do you believe are most compatible with or antagonistic toward Christian faith or theology? Why?

2. Choose one or two of the illustrative concerns examined in chapter 5 and discuss it or them further. Identify the different values, principles, theories, or approaches that are invoked during the discussion.

3. As a Christian, what do you believe would constitute a "good death"? What types of moral acts would best help achieve or implement your description? Why?

4. Given the different approaches to moral reflection and discernment summarized in chapter 4, as well as the illustrative concerns described in chapter 5, is there any additional advice or counsel you would care to offer to any or all the characters in the stories of Mary, Steve, Helen, and Bob and Ann?

5. If you should be, or are now, faced with a life-threatening condition with limited time left, how has the discussion in Part 3 helped, or failed to help, in making decisions affecting your care and dying? What other considerations do you consider appropriate?

Part 4
Toward a Doxology of Death

6
Epilogue

When, as Christians, we gather to worship we often sing the familiar words of the Doxology:

> Praise God, from whom all blessings flow,
> Praise Him, all creatures here below;
> Praise Him above, ye heavenly hosts;
> Praise Father, Son, and Holy Ghost.

Or as a more modern version puts it:

> Praise God, from whom all blessings flow;
> Praise Christ the Word in flesh born low;
> Praise Holy Spirit evermore;
> One God, Triune, whom we adore.

Both versions capture and portray a fitting response to the gift and loan of life which includes suffering, dying, and death. For God embraces our entire being, or as Karl Barth once observed: "All of us are somewhere on the notable way from the cradle to the grave, which is also notable at each of its many stations."[1] A doxology is, then, a fitting offering of praise and glory to God; a central part of our life and worship.

The doxology, however, is more than a song we sing on Sunday morning or, even more appropriately, at a funeral. Giving God praise and glory marks the pattern of our faith. We give thanks and offer our gratitude to God who, in Christ and through the Holy Spirit, creates, redeems, and sustains our lives. As Christians, how we live, suffer, and die should be doxological.

Thinking of life as a blessing, gift, and loan will surely seem odd and out of place in our contemporary age. We are coming to believe that life is merely a result of biological processes, physical material we may manipulate, and has only whatever meaning and value we choose to assign. There is a prevalent presumption that life is largely what we make of it, a possession or commodity to control as we please.

To insist, however, that life is a blessing, gift, and loan is a reminder that our lives are not our own. The language we use to describe life, as well as our lives, will in turn shape how we respond to its joys and sorrows. If life is thought to be a possession or commodity, then suffering, dying, and death are inevitable problems that we will nonetheless try to ignore, evade, or eliminate. If life is a gift and loan, then suffering, dying, and death are marks of God's creative, redemptive, and sustaining ways of ordering the world. It is God, then, and not our survival that should capture our attention and devotion. "Properly understood," Stanley Hauerwas writes, "the language of 'gift of life' is not meant to direct our attention to the gift, but rather to the nature of the giver and the conditions under which it is given. Life is not a gift as an end, in and of itself."[2]

As Christians we give God glory and praise for the gift and loan of life. The natural processes which order the world through a creative and sustaining dance between life and death are parts of this gift, and we are, in turn, called to use our particular lives as loans entrusted to our safekeeping.

Yet the gift and loan of life is not simply a collection of impersonal forces and processes. We are not deists but Christians who offer doxologies to a personal God; the God of Sarah and Abraham, Rebecca and Isaac, Rachel and Jacob. We give God praise and thanks for the lives of particular persons, our own and those of friends and loved ones. The triune God whom we worship and serve loves, enjoys, and suffers with the creatures.

A doxological life, however, does not ignore or soften the reality of suffering and death. Even while giving God praise and glory for the gift and loan of life we must also acknowledge death. The physical suffering that may accompany dying cannot be ignored, explained away, or embraced as being good for any reason or purpose. The emotional and spiritual pain we feel when a friend or loved one dies creates an emptiness that will not be filled, or, to paraphrase Hauerwas, a silence that cannot be named.[3]

Nor does a doxological faith protect one from the tragic circumstances that may shape the deaths of particular persons. A young son or daughter dying of cancer, the death of a spouse in an automobile accident, a murdered relative, or a friend committing suicide strike us as being particularly tragic because we can make no sense of them. In the face of such deaths we feel not only a deep sadness but also indignation and outrage that these people have been denied the possibility of a long and full life.

A Christian faith formed in the doxological pattern of giving praise and glory to God does not imply we must deny that death is evil; it works its woe in the world. As the Psalms of lament demonstrate, reactions of sadness, anger, and bitterness are also natural, human, and religious responses to death. As Christians we do not confront death with either quiet resignation or a loving embrace. To make our peace with this final enemy is not the same thing as unconditional surrender. Because of our faith and hope in Christ, our suffering and grief may become holy and redemptive. For God not only creates and sustains our lives but also shares and redeems our suffering and death.

Consequently, we accept that death, including our own, is part of God's natural ordering of the world. Without death, creation cannot be sustained and redeemed. All mortal creatures, including ourselves and those we love, have a beginning and an end. Under certain circumstances, then, the end of life is not a tragedy to be endured, but accepted, as it was at its beginning, as a gift and blessing. There comes a time when resisting death must and should cease. Although death remains, this side of eternity, the final enemy, we face it with a peace and confidence that it has already been vanquished in Christ. To offer a doxology in death's long shadow is to give thanks to God for the gift of life, and also to proclaim our hope that when as a loan it is collected it will be neither destroyed nor forgotten. We offer praise and glory that through death our lives are resurrected into the eternal life of God.

Earlier it was observed that behind all our theological beliefs and moral pondering there are people with unique hopes and dreams. Consequently, our reflection began with four stories of dying and death, and it is fitting that in concluding we return to them. For we need to see whether a doxological orientation can help us perceive the suffering, dying, and grief of these stories in a holy and redemptive manner.

For Mary, as well as for her doctors and family, it must be determined whether further life-prolonging treatments represent a responsible stewardship of her life, or a sinful attempt to do too much. The issue is not to judge whether the resulting quality of Mary's life would be worth the medical effort, but a faithful response in light of her imminent death. If it seems likely that life-prolonging treatments can enable Mary to fulfill the purposes for which she was created—namely, to love and enjoy God—then they should be pursued. If not, then the time of fighting against death has properly come to an end. In either case it is time for her family, friends, and those providing her care to maintain a faithful presence that her healing and suffering might be redemptive. It is also in such a faithful vigil that the way is prepared for making Mary's death doxological. For praise and glory is offered to God not only as thanks for the life she has lived but also as a demonstration of hope so that the resulting grief may be made holy and redemptive.

Steve, the young man dying of AIDS, faces the bleak prospect of a tragic death. In the face of unacceptable parental demands and the inability of his companion to provide the care he will require, suicide becomes an option to avoid an impending and unwanted abandonment. Yet to commit suicide under these circumstances would be a failure to resist the temptation of settling for too little. Steve should be helped to exercise a responsible stewardship of his life so that his death may be timely and fitting. This will require a faithful presence, perhaps largely by people who do not know and have little in common with Steve and his companion.

This story presents two distinct challenges. For Steve, the challenge is to accept the care and comfort of strangers. In dying we learn that our lives are not our own, and we share a vulnerability when life is literally at the mercy of others. There is also a challenge to the church to offer hospitality to the stranger. To keep a faithful presence with those we do not know or who are "not like us" is to work with God in healing the wounds that divide and fragment creation; acts of compassion that help ease its groaning, if but a little. It is in giving and receiving care and comfort between strangers that suffering may find its redemptive healing.

Helen, the gifted scholar with Alzheimer's disease, presents potentially the most tragic situation. Her impending loss of independence and sense of dignity means that her life is no longer worth living. For Helen life is neither a gift nor loan, but a possession to be done with as she pleases. Consequently, stewardship of one's life, or resisting the temptations of doing too much or settling for too little, are not pertinent considerations. Helen has chosen to abandon the living before she is abandoned while dying and will request the assistance of a physician to accomplish her desire.

This story again presents two challenges. The church needs to cling tenaciously to the language of life as a gift and loan despite the fact that it grows increasingly meaningless in a secular society and is often misused by political causes we do not endorse. Yet without a countervailing voice the presumption that life is a commodity, along with its accompanying moral prescriptions, will only grow more dominant. In the name of individual sovereignty even matters of life and death will be confined to fulfilling personal wants and desires as a form of consumer rights and behavior. Although Helen is not an evil or wicked person, she does personify a prevalent orientation and belief in need of repentance and conversion.

The other challenge involves the practice of medicine. The church needs to remind doctors that they are not simply dispensers of services to customers. Physicians are also members of a moral community who practice the art of healing. The legitimate instructions and requests of patients should be respected and honored, but medicine also has a moral obligation to assist the dying in exercising their stewardship of life. Even in the midst of dying there is a need for genuine and compassionate evangelism; otherwise suffering and grief remain pointless and unredeemed.

The story of Bob and Ann is complex and heartrending. We can empathize with Bob's dismay, anger, and frustration with a medical practice that will not allow Ann to die. Yet, if he takes matters into his own hands to rectify the situation, he will fail to exercise his stewardship of life in a responsible manner. Ann's life is not his to take. Although his wish to end her life is motivated by his love and compassion, it will not correct or redeem the consequences of medical efforts to do too much. In addition, the act he is contemplating could lead to his forced abandonment of his children at a time when they may need him the most. Our commitments to the dying do not supersede our duties to others.

In this instance the church is called to both a prophetic and a pastoral ministry. Although Ann's life does not belong to her husband, neither does it belong to the state. Our lives are not our own, nor are they owned by Caesar. Prophetically the church must insist that there are limits to political authority, particularly in matters of life and death. To transgress these limits is to usurp a sovereignty over life that properly belongs to God. It is ironic that with a growing popular perception of life as a commodity and personal possession we increasingly turn to public agencies to determine how we regulate and dispose of this property. Determining the fitting time of Ann's death is a problem better resolved in the relationship between her family and physicians than in courts and legislatures.

Pastorally the church is called to offer Bob and his family a faithful presence that is both patient and enduring. Ann's medical treatment has effectively suspended the dying process. Consequently, the possibility for redemptive healing and suffering has also been placed on hold, and a time for a holy and redemptive grieving delayed. It is again ironic that medical treatments designed to enhance the lives of patients are used in ways to discourage a redemptive healing, suffering, and grief among the survivors. Under these circumstances it is foolish to pretend that we are not vainly resisting a providential ordering of the world where life runs its course to death. It is even difficult to invoke petitionary prayer, for how can God's will be done when there is little respect or consideration for ending mortal life in a timely manner? The church needs to embrace Bob and his family with a faithful and patient presence so they will not be abandoned to a lonely vigil.

At the very least, a doxological orientation toward death suggests that the church needs to recover a ministry of healing. This does not mean that Christians should adopt practices intended to supplant, complement, or enhance medical treatments and techniques. As already mentioned, a ministry of healing in the name of Christ is concerned not with physical phenomena but with a redeeming or transformation of our suffering and grief. The church of Jesus Christ is simply not interested in mastering medical magic whether its source is technological or supernatural.

For too long the church has forsaken healing as a part of its mission and ministry. Retreating into the comfortable fiction that suffering and dying are medical problems best solved by physicians, it has concentrated on helping individuals cope with death. Such an artificial division will not do. As Christians we do not worship a God who is only the Lord of our souls, but the One who creates, redeems, and sustains our lives in their entirety.

A doxological orientation toward death beckons Christians to once again care for the dying. To die is not necessarily a private or lonely affair. We often avoid the dying in the name of honoring their need for rest and solitude. Yet genuine rest and solitude are best supported when the dying are embraced rather than ignored or abandoned by the community of faith. As Kenneth Vaux suggests, there is much the church can do in caring for the dying:

> When the process of sickness and dying begins in one of our congregations, let us put into motion this process of helping, consoling, grappling for meaning, providing meals, caring for

children and guests who arrive from around the country, and just distracting to allow relief. If the home is a setting that is comfortable, let us bring the pastoral care of the congregation to that person, offering prayer, consolation, "good-time sharing," gratitude for life, and provision of any particular need. If, as is increasingly the case, appropriate home situations do not exist, let us set up parish houses, perhaps even with modest medical and nursing provision (church clinics are a good start in this direction), where persons may receive the grace of death in the presence of God and the members of the community of faith.[4]

Our caring for the dying is always rooted in compassion. Although there is a connection between sin, suffering, and death, a deathbed is not the time or place to sort out the cause-and-effect relationships of specific acts. It is, rather, a time and place to emphasize forgiveness and grace so the way is prepared for redemptive healing, suffering, and grief. A doxological orientation, the giving of praise and glory to God, is concerned with mercy and love rather than with judgment and guilt.

Consequently, we treat those who must make decisions about their own impending deaths with a deep sense of compassion and sympathy, "taken in its literal sense of *sympatheia*—'suffering with.'"[5] We help them exercise their stewardship of life, but always with gentle kindness rather than a demanding and prescriptive attitude. The same compassion and sympathy are offered as well to those who are directly affected by the decisions made by the dying. As part of our ministry of healing we must not forget that death can also work its evil upon survivors, and those left behind must not be abandoned.

It is in worship, however, that a doxological orientation forms and shapes us as a community. It is when we gather to worship that we most directly give praise and glory to God. Indeed we worship for no other purpose than to offer gratitude and thanksgiving to God for the blessings and tender mercies that are bestowed upon creation. It is in the holy presence of God that the whole communion of saints is gathered and sanctified, that the healthy and sick, the living and dead, are made one in Christ. It is in worship that we find the strength and capacity to die in the same way we live as Christians: in lives claimed by God and molded in the virtues of faith, hope, and love.

It is also in worship that we may honestly confess that the reality of death is surrounded by an enigmatic but certain hope. As Paul reminds us, "We see puzzling reflections in a mirror" and our "knowledge now is partial."[6] To place our hope in the resurrection of Jesus Christ means we cannot speak precisely. We do not know exactly what being raised from the dead into the life of God entails or how it will be accomplished. Our words will fail our attempts, and at best all we can offer are suggestive metaphors and images. We see puzzling reflections; we know only in part.

Yet our hope is certain. Jesus Christ was raised from the dead. Easter is the beginning and end of our faith, for the fate of Jesus' mortal life is ours as well: "The sign of the resurrection of Jesus affirms that God does something new for his creation in the face of the finality of death. He creates new possibilities of life and relationships where, from a human point of view, life has come to an end."[7] Regardless of how puzzling the details of our hope may be, we do see, and our partial knowledge will someday be whole and complete.

It is because of a doxological orientation that we believe God creates, redeems, and sustains our lives because of a love we cannot fully comprehend or express. Our lives, then, can be understood as gifts and loans of love. In response the words of Charles Wesley offer a fitting invocation:

> Love divine, all loves excelling,
> Joy of heav'n, to earth come down,
> Fix in us thy humble dwelling,
> All thy faithful mercies crown.
> Jesu, thou art all compassion,
> Pure unbounded love thou art;
> Visit us with thy salvation,
> Enter every trembling heart.[8]

At the end of our lives we remain embraced by God's love, a love that uses death to order and sustain creation toward its consummation and complete redemption. It is a love that makes possible a hope for a time when God, in the words of Julian of Norwich, "shall make all well that is not well."[9] In God's creative, redemptive, and sustaining love, death becomes enfolded in the gift and blessing of life. Even as our lives end we may, again using Wesley's words, offer a fitting doxology and benediction:

> Finish then thy new creation,
> Pure and sinless let us be;
> Let us see thy great salvation,
> Perfectly restored in thee:
> Changed from glory into glory,
> Till in heav'n we take our place,
> Till we cast our crowns before thee,
> Lost in wonder, love, and praise![10]

Appendix 1
Resolution
The Rights and Responsibilities of Christians Regarding Human Death

Background

We all eventually must die. When death does come, we hope that it will be swift, that we will not experience prolonged suffering, and that our dignity will remain intact. There have always been possible circumstances involving death when these desires are not fulfilled. The concern has been intensified by recent medical advances in which medical machines can indefinitely keep people "alive" in critical care units under conditions of intense, undignified suffering. Advanced life support measures such as cardiopulmonary resuscitation, mechanical ventilators, renal dialysis, renal, cardiac, lung and bone marrow transplants, and artificial hearts are no longer futuristic treatments. It is in this context that euthanasia and suicide need to be examined.

The term *euthanasia* now refers both to putting to death the incurably ill and to the withdrawing or withholding of artificial means used mainly to prolong life. A related concern is suicide, the taking of one's own life, as a response to a painful, lingering death or the prospect of a debilitating or terminal disease.

Euthanasic legislation has been enacted in a number of states. There are two general kinds of legislation in effect or under consideration: validating provisions to permit instructions for terminal care, e.g., "living wills," and protecting the right of patients to refuse treatment. This legislation does not deal adequately with all contingencies.

Ethical and Theological Issues

More important are the ethical and theological issues. One of the underlying moral conflicts centers on the patient's desire to control what happens to his or her body and the family and health care professionals' commitment to preserve life. For example, sometimes a dying person is in continuous pain that cannot be alleviated by medication, except in amounts which may hasten death. Furthermore, improved diet and health care, disease prevention, and health precautions have extended life expectancy for many into a much longer period of advanced years of utter helplessness.

The Religious Perspective

In light of these perplexities, what is our response? Our Christian perspective is that life is a gift, sourced in God, and that Christians are called to a life of freedom and responsibility as evidenced in the teachings and life of Christ. Our covenantal faith requires that we serve the ends of fullness of life—in body and spirit, mind and human relationships—to the extent possible. Death is an inevitable part of every life process. It is not our enemy, but a part of the life cycle which we attribute to God as Creator. This present issue is about the manner of death and attitudes toward death when there is no hope for recovery to any significant degree. We affirm individual freedom and responsibility to make choices in these matters. It is not claimed that euthanasia is the Christian position, but that the right to choose is a legitimate Christian decision. It is contended that governmental powers and entrenched custom have made life and death decisions, closing off options which more properly belong to individuals and families.

Words from the Ninth General Synod of the United Church of Christ are helpful as we consider issues which have arisen since 1973:

> Theology is necessarily a being theology. It intends to relate our tradition to present and changing concerns. It searches for the will of God known and to be made known to us.
>
> The supreme value in our religious heritage is derived from God the giver of personal wholeness, freedom, integrity, and dignity. When illness takes away those abilities we associate with full personhood, leaving one so impaired that what is most valuable and precious is gone, we may feel that the mere continuance of the body by machines or drugs is a violation of the person.

Text of Resolution

WHEREAS, we live in an era of complex biomedical technologies, with various means to maintain or prolong physical life and postpone inevitable death;

WHEREAS, there are ever-increasing anxieties about a prolonged dying process with irreversible deterioration, and its potentially devastating effects on the dignity of the dying person, the emotional and physical well-being of families, as well as the responsible Christian stewardship of resources;

WHEREAS, technology advances more quickly than public policy, and public opinion is often ahead of legislative enactment;

WHEREAS, individuals have increasing responsibilities in these life-and-death decisions, but often lack adequate information regarding available options;

WHEREAS, life is sourced in God, and recognizing that our faith calls for commitment and work for the quality of human life with mercy, justice, and truth;

WHEREAS, affirming that the gift of abundant life is more than the avoidance of death, and that over-regard for the body, without proper concern for the needs of the person or the human spirit, can become a kind of biological idolatry, we are convinced that what is required is a balanced appreciation of the whole person;

WHEREAS, General Synod 12 of the United Church of Christ has supported the legal recognition of living wills and General Synod 9 addressed the rights and responsibilities of Christians regarding human death; and

WHEREAS, we support the right and responsibility of individuals to choose their own destiny, and recognize the need for safeguards to protect persons who cannot make life-and-death choices for themselves.

THEREFORE, BE IT RESOLVED, the Eighteenth General Synod supports the right of individuals, their designees, and their families to make decisions regarding human death and dying.

BE IT FURTHER RESOLVED, the Eighteenth General Synod affirms the right of individuals to die with dignity and not have their lives unnecessarily prolonged by extraordinary measures if so chosen.

BE IT FURTHER RESOLVED, the Eighteenth General Synod calls on Christians to offer love, compassion, and understanding to those who are faced with difficult life-ending decisions.

BE IT FURTHER RESOLVED, the Eighteenth General Synod calls upon the churches to study and discuss life-ending issues with resources provided by the United Church Board for Homeland Ministries, the United Church Board for World Ministries, the Office for Church in Society and the Council for Health and Human Service Ministries.

BE IT FURTHER RESOLVED, the Eighteenth General Synod calls upon the United Church Board for Homeland Ministries, the United Church Board for World Ministries, the Office for Church in Society and the Council for Health and Human Service Ministries to report to General Synod 19.

BE IT FURTHER RESOLVED, the Eighteenth General Synod encourages the enactment of legislation safeguarding these rights, including the rights of those who are unable to make decisions for themselves.

Subject to the availability of funds.

91-GS-44 VOTED: General Synod Eighteen adopts the Resolution "The Rights and Responsibilities of Christians Regarding Human Death."

Appendix 2
Glossary

Advance directives   Instructions indicating what type of medical treatments should be performed if a person becomes incompetent because of a terminal illness or debilitating accident. Ideally, advance care directives are formal documents that have been reviewed and discussed by the patient, physician, and surrogate. Advance directives are also referred to as "advance care directives" and "living wills."

Autonomy   The right to make free, informed, and uncoerced decisions affecting the course and fate of one's own life. Autonomy in a medical setting is the right of a competent person to be informed of medical options regarding an illness and to choose which, if any, will be used.

Beneficence   The moral obligation of a physician to perform or authorize only such treatments as will potentially benefit the patient.

Bioethics   An interdisciplinary study of a wide range of moral concerns associated with contemporary health care. A variety of methods for moral reflection and discernment are employed by bioethicists.

Brain death   Irreversible cessation of all vital functions of the brain; used as a legal criterion that death has occurred.

Casuistry   A method of moral reflection and discernment that attempts to attain practical wisdom. Attention is focused on concrete or particular situations rather than general or abstract moral principles. The goal is to obtain agreement on what should be done in a particular set of circumstances regardless of the different and conflicting reasons used to support the decision.

Deontological ethics An ethical theory stressing the central role of universal principles from which specific duties are derived. Moral conduct results when the right duty is performed regardless of the circumstances or consequences.

Euthanasia The literal meaning of the word is a "good, noble, or merciful death." In contemporary use it refers to various medical treatments which either hasten or cause the death of a dying patient. Passive measures either allow or hasten death, while active forms directly cause death. Voluntary euthanasia is euthanasia desired and requested by a person who is competent to make such a decision. Involuntary euthanasia is euthanasia that is performed against the wishes of a person. Nonvoluntary euthanasia occurs when the wishes of an individual are not known.

Hospice A form of care for the dying in which the primary goals are to provide comfort and control pain rather than extend longevity. Hospice care may be provided in a central location or in-home.

Incompetent patient An individual who is not able to make decisions regarding his or her medical treatment. Incompetent patients include infants and young children, the severely retarded, comatose persons, and individuals suffering severe dementia or other profound mental disorders.

Informed consent Consent given by a patient, or surrogate, before any medical procedure is performed. For consent to be fully informed, the physician must disclose full and complete information regarding the illness, medical options, and potential consequences.

Life-prolonging treatment A medical procedure or intervention intended to extend the life of a dying patient. The treatments employed range from simple and routine to highly experimental and technologically sophisticated.

Narrative ethics Also known as "virtue ethics" or an "ethics of character." This approach to moral reflection and discernment asserts that our moral character is shaped by the virtues we practice, which in turn gain their normative content from authoritative stories or narrative structures. Christians, for example, practice the virtues of faith, hope, and love so that they will respond in faithful, hopeful, and loving ways.

Nonmaleficence The moral obligation of a doctor to never intentionally harm a patient.

Persistent vegetative state The condition of an individual who is unconscious but whose respiration and other vital functions continue without medical assistance. Nutrition and hydration are provided through tubes attached to the stomach. Depending on age or other health factors a person may continue to live for an extended period of time under these conditions.

Physician-assisted suicide Ending one's own life with the assistance of a doctor or health care professional. The assistance is provided in response to a request by a dying or chronically ill patient who is usually seeking a relatively quick and painless death to avoid having to endure prolonged suffering or anticipated deterioration.

Quality of life A belief or claim that the value of a human life is derived from its relative quality. According to this view, individuals must determine what constitutes an acceptable level of quality and make medical decisions accordingly, including ending a life if desired. There are both religious and secular versions of a quality of life position.

Sanctity of life A belief or claim that human life is sacred and should be accorded respect and protection. According to this view, medicine should try to prolong the life, or at least never hasten the death, of a dying person, except in rare circumstances. There are both religious and secular versions of a sanctity of life position.

Surrogate An individual authorized to make decisions regarding the medical care and treatment of an incompetent dying person. A surrogate is expected to make decisions that either reflect the wishes and desires of the patient or are in the patient's best interests.

Teleological ethics An ethical theory holding that an act is judged to be good or bad based on the consequences it produces. Utilitarianism, a teleological form of moral reasoning, argues that what should be done is what would maximize the greatest good for the greatest number in a particular situation.

Withholding treatment A decision to not use certain medical procedures to treat a terminal or related illness or condition. A competent patient has the right to refuse medical treatment at any time. Withholding treatment may also occur as a form of passive euthanasia for competent or incompetent patients.

Appendix 3
Resources

Organizations

The Hastings Center carries out educational and research programs on ethical issues in medicine, the life sciences, and the professions. The center publishes a journal as well as reports on a variety of bioethical topics. Address: 255 Elm Road, Briarcliff Manor, New York 10510.

The Joseph and Rose Kennedy Institute of Ethics is a research and teaching center of Georgetown University. Its purpose is to offer moral perspective on major policy issues, reflecting a wide variety of academic disciplines and interests. The institute publishes a journal and sponsors a variety of conferences and educational events relating to various bioethical topics. Address: Poulton Hall, 37th and P Streets, N.W., Georgetown University, Washington, DC 20057.

The Park Ridge Center explores the relationships between health, faith, and ethics. It sponsors programs of research, publishing, and education which stress the bearing of religious beliefs on questions that confront people as they search for health and encounter illness. The center promotes ethical reflection on a wide range of health-related issues, and its programs and publications reflect a breadth of religious, cultural, intellectual, and professional perspectives. Address: 211 East Ontario, Suite 800, Chicago, Illinois 60611.

The Society for Health and Human Values is an international organization that promotes the teaching of the humanities in the formal education of health care professionals. In addition to its publications the Society sponsors an annual meeting, workshops, and interdisciplinary consultations and discussions. Address: 6728 Old McLean Village Drive, McLean, Virginia 22101.

Choice in Dying, Inc., 200 Varick St., New York, N.Y. 10014-4810. (1-800-989-WILL). A national not-for-profit organization dedicated to protecting the rights and serving the needs of dying patients and their families. Advocates patients' rights to make their own decisions about medical treatment and to receive compassionate and dignified care at the end of life. Educates the general public, health care professionals, and lawmakers to the needs of people who are dying. Develops educational publications and videos. Has current information on state-specific advance directives.

Periodicals and Journals

Hastings Center Report. Published six times a year by the Hastings Center. Offers general articles on a wide range of bioethical issues and health care topics. Address: 225 Elm Road, Briarcliff Manor, New York 10510.

The Journal of Medicine and Philosophy. Published six times a year by Kluwer Academic Publishers Group. Provides a forum for bioethics and the philosophy of medicine. Articles are usually academic and technical. Address: Kluwer Academic Publishers Group, P.O. Box 322, 3300 AH Dordrecht, Netherlands, or P.O. Box 358, Accord Station, Hingham, Massachusetts 02018-0358.

Kennedy Institute of Ethics Journal. Published quarterly by the Kennedy Institute of Ethics. This academic and interdisciplinary journal is dedicated to publishing articles dealing with social, ethical, and public policy aspects of bioethics and related areas of applied ethics. Address: Journal Publishing Division, Johns Hopkins University Press, 2715 North Charles Street, Baltimore, Maryland 21218-4319.

Second Opinion. Published quarterly by the Park Ridge Center. Offers articles reflecting a wide range of perspectives relating to health, faith, and ethics. Articles are aimed at a diverse but educated public, and authors are encouraged to "not write for the six specialists in your field, but rather for the general reader." Address: 211 East Ontario, Suite 800, Chicago, Illinois 60611.

Trends in Health Care, Law and Ethics. Published quarterly by BioEthics Consulting, Inc. Presents articles relating to contemporary issues in health care. Primary focus is on controversial ethical and legal issues. Address: P.O. Box 896, Piscataway, New Jersey 08855-0896.

Legal Issues and Concerns

There are a variety of federal and state laws and statutes governing the medical care of the dying. These codes are subject to periodic legislative change and judicial review. Local attorneys or legal organizations should be consulted as needed. In addition, the following organizations and resources may be helpful:

For general information, contact the Council for Health and Human Service Ministries of the United Church of Christ (CHHSM), 700 Prospect Avenue, Cleveland, Ohio 44115.

CHHSM and the United Church of Christ Chaplains in Health Care have also published a booklet, *Making End-of-Life Decisions: United Church of Christ Perspectives*, 1993. It contains summaries of various medical, legal, ethical, and practical concerns as well as a listing of professional organizations associated with end-of-life concerns. A copy may be obtained from the CHHSM address listed above.

The following books may also be consulted:

Colen, B. D. *The Essential Guide to a Living Will: How to Protect Your Right to Refuse Medical Treatment*. Englewood Cliffs, N.J.: Prentice Hall, 1991.

Collins, Evan R., and Doron Weber. *The Complete Guide to Living Wills: How to Safeguard Your Treatment Choices*. New York: Bantam Books, 1991.

Smith, Bradley E., and Jess Brallier. *Write Your Own Living Will*. New York: Crown Publishers, 1991.

Urofsky, Melvin I. *Letting Go: Death, Dying, and the Law*. New York: Charles Scribner's Sons, 1993.

Miscellaneous Books

Beauchamp, Tom L., and James F. Childress. *Principles of Biomedical Ethics*. New York: Oxford University Press, 1979. A classic introductory text on bioethics.

Fiddes, Paul S. *The Creative Suffering of God*. Oxford, U.K.: Clarendon Press, 1988. Provides a survey of recent theological thought on the suffering of God and the implications for Christian faith.

Gunton, Colin E. *Christ and Creation*. Grand Rapids, Mich.: William B. Eerdmans, 1992. A theological investigation of the relationship between creation and redemption.

Hamel, Ron P., ed. *Choosing Death: Active Euthanasia, Religion, and the Public Debate*. Philadelphia: Trinity Press International, 1991. A collection of essays that examine the morality of euthanasia from a variety of religious and ethical perspectives. The book was commissioned by the Park Ridge Center.

Hauerwas, Stanley. *Naming the Silences: God, Medicine, and the Problem of Suffering*. Grand Rapids, Mich.: William B. Eerdmans, 1990. A theological account of the problem of suffering in the context of contemporary medicine.

———. *Suffering Presence: Theological Reflections on Medi-*

cine, the Mentally Handicapped, and the Church. Notre Dame, Ind.: University of Notre Dame Press, 1986. An account of medicine, suffering, dying, and death from the perspective of a narrative theologian.

Kilner, John F. *Life on the Line: Ethics, Aging, Ending Patients' Lives, and Allocating Vital Resources.* Grand Rapids, Mich.: William B. Eerdmans, 1992. A theological and ethical analysis of issues relating to medical care at the end of life.

Macklin, Ruth. *Mortal Choices: Ethical Dilemmas in Modern Medicine.* Boston: Houghton Mifflin, 1987. An introduction and overview of contemporary bioethics.

May, William F. *The Physician's Covenant: Images of the Healer in Medical Ethics.* Philadelphia: The Westminster Press, 1983. An ethical overview and critique of the role of physicians in health care.

O'Donovan, Oliver. *Resurrection and Moral Order: An Outline for Evangelical Ethics.* Grand Rapids, Mich.: William B. Eerdmans, 1986. A highly detailed theological account of the ethical implications regarding the relationship among the doctrines of creation, redemption, and eschatology.

Polkinghorne, John. *Science and Providence: God's Interaction with the World.* London: SPCK, 1989. An accessible introduction to theological thought in an age of science. Some of the principal themes addressed include providence, miracles, evil, prayer, time, and hope.

Rachels, James. *The End of Life: Euthanasia and Morality.* Oxford: Oxford University Press, 1986. A philosophical argument in favor of "liberal" euthanasia laws and policies. There is also a strong and extensive critique of the sanctity of life position as well as traditional Christian moral teachings.

Ramsey, Paul. *The Patient as Person: Explorations in Medical Ethics.* New Haven, Ct.: Yale University Press, 1970. Although some of the issues addressed are now dated, this remains a classic theological critique of medicine from a deontological perspective.

Shannon, Thomas A., ed. *Bioethics.* 3d ed. Mahwah, N.J.: Paulist Press, 1987. An introductory anthology covering such topics as children with severe handicaps, death and dying, ethical dilemmas in obtaining informed consent, and the allocation of scarce resources.

Thomasma, David C., and Glenn C. Graber. *Euthanasia: Toward an Ethical Social Policy*. New York: Continuum, 1990. Examines various public policy dilemmas and issues regarding euthanasia.

Vaux, Kenneth L. *Death Ethics: Religious and Cultural Values in Prolonging and Ending Life*. Philadelphia: Trinity Press International, 1992. A comprehensive inquiry into ethical and religious issues associated with dying and death.

Wennberg, Robert N. *Terminal Choices: Euthanasia, Suicide, and the Right to Die*. Grand Rapids, Mich.: William B. Eerdmans, 1989. A theological and philosophical investigation and analysis of the various dimensions of suicide and euthanasia.

Notes

Preface

1. See Appendix 1.
2. Resolution titled "The Rights and Responsibilities of Christians Regarding Human Death" (91-GS-44), adopted at U.C.C. General Synod Eighteen, p. 3. It should be noted that these resolutions do not address related topics of unexpected or violent deaths.

1. Overview

1. David C. Thomasma and Glenn C. Graber, *Euthanasia: Toward an Ethical Social Policy* (New York: Continuum, 1991), 85.
2. Ibid., 86.
3. Paul Ramsey, *The Patient as Person: Explorations in Medical Ethics* (New Haven, Conn.: Yale University Press, 1970), 59.
4. This is why an anencephalic infant cannot be used as a source for infant organ transplants.
5. William F. May, *The Physician's Covenant: Images of the Healer in Medical Ethics* (Philadelphia: Westminster Press, 1983), 32.
6. Ibid.
7. Ibid., 33.
8. Ibid.
9. The origin of the "right to die" movement in the United States can be traced back to the early twentieth century.
10. Thomasma and Graber, *Euthanasia*, 2.

11. Robert N. Wennberg, *Terminal Choices: Euthanasia, Suicide, and the Right to Die* (Grand Rapids, Mich.: Wm. B. Eerdmans, 1989), 9.
12. Ibid.
13. Ibid.
14. This is why physicians are not asked to serve as executioners, even in states where the method of capital punishment is through lethal injection. A physician is present to verify death, but the injection itself is performed by the executioner.
15. Sidney H. Wanzer et al., "The Physician's Responsibility toward Hopelessly Ill Patients: A Second Look," in *Quality of Life: The New Medical Dilemma*, ed. James J. Walter and Thomas A. Shannon (New York: Paulist Press, 1990), 289.
16. For some, sanctity also extends to other life forms.
17. James J. Walter and Thomas A. Shannon, "Foreword: An Overview of 'Quality of Life,'" in *Quality of Life*, ed. Walter and Shannon, 1.
18. Courtney S. Campbell, "Religious Ethics and Active Euthanasia in a Pluralistic Society," *Kennedy Institute of Ethics Journal* 2:3 (1992): 255.
19. Stanley Hauerwas, *Suffering Presence: Theological Reflections on Medicine, the Mentally Handicapped, and the Church* (Notre Dame, Ind.: University of Notre Dame Press, 1986), 16-17.
20. May, *Physician's Covenant*, 143.
21. Hauerwas, *Suffering Presence*, 6.

2. Changing Christian Attitudes toward Dying and Death

1. It is interesting to note that such terms as "death," "dead," "die," "died," and "dying" are used 1,271 times in the NRSV.
2. "Leprosy" is a general designation that includes a wide variety of diseases, usually associated with eruptive skin disorders. Exile or ostracism was imposed because it was thought that leprosy represented an uncleanliness that could infect the community.
3. An act designed to mollify the anger or wrath of God.
4. For a summary of biblical reasons why suffering and death occur, see Erhard S. Gerstenberger and Wolfgang Schrage, *Suffering*, trans. John E. Steely (Nashville: Abingdon, 1980), 103-16, 188-242.
5. Job 1:21.
6. See 2 Kings 5:1-14.
7. Gerstenberger and Schrage, *Suffering*, 207.
8. Ibid., 215.
9. Ibid., 204-5.
10. Wennberg has observed that "the term 'suicide' was introduced into the English language in 1651 by Walter Charleton in order to make available a

more neutral and less judgmental term for acts of self-killing which until then had been described as 'destroying oneself,' 'murdering oneself,' and 'slaughtering oneself'—all phrases that convey firm disapproval" (*Terminal Choices*, 17).

11. As quoted in Wennberg, *Terminal Choice*, 45. For a discussion of Barth's position on suicide, see Karl Barth, *Ethics*, ed. Dietrich Braun, trans. Geoffrey Bromiley (New York: Seabury Press, 1981), 47-48.
12. It is uncertain whether or not the death of Sampson should be included as a sixth case. It is unclear if he intended his own death or if it was an unwanted side effect of his desire to kill the Philistines. See Judges 16:23-31.
13. See Judges 9:50-56.
14. Wennberg, *Terminal Choices*, 47.
15. Judges 9:56.
16. See 1 Samuel 31:1-13, and 1 Chronicles 10:1-14. Cf. 2 Samuel 1:1-16.
17. 1 Chronicles 10:13. This commentary is not found in the parallel descriptions of Saul's death in 1 Samuel 31. It is also interesting to note that in 2 Samuel 1, Saul's suicide attempt fails and he is killed, at his request, by a soldier. After reporting his deed to David, the new king, the soldier is in turn executed for destroying "the Lord's anointed" (1:14). One can only speculate whether the same moral judgment would have applied to Saul had he been successful in his attempt to commit suicide, for his proper burial and ritual mourning seemed premised on his being slain in battle. See 2 Samuel 1:19-27.
18. See 1 Kings 16:15-20.
19. Wennberg, *Terminal Choices*, 47.
20. 1 Kings 16:19.
21. See 2 Samuel 17:21-23.
22. Hans Wilhelm Hertzberg, *I and II Samuel: A Commentary*, trans. J. S. Bowden (Philadelphia: Westminster Press, 1960), 353.
23. 2 Samuel 17:23.
24. See Matthew 27:3-10. Cf. Acts 1:15-20.
25. Matthew reports that Judas "went and hanged himself" (27:5). Acts, however, records that he fell "headlong" (1:18) in a field that he had purchased with thirty pieces of silver. What is also not clear is whether the thirty pieces of silver were used by the priests to purchase a "potter's field," as recorded in Matthew, or if Judas used the money to purchase some property as stated in Acts. In either case, the land became known to subsequent generations as a "field of blood." For discussions regarding the death of Judas, see W. F. Albright, and C. S. Mann, *Matthew* (Garden City, N.Y.: Doubleday, 1971), 340-41, and Johannes Munck, *The Acts of the Apostles* (Garden City, N.Y.: Doubleday, 1967), 9-12.
26. Matthew 27:4.
27. Acts 1:18.
28. Wennberg, *Terminal Choices*, 48.

29. Ibid.
30. Jonah 4:8. See also 4:5-11.
31. Job 2:9.
32. Job 2:10.
33. For example, see Philippians 1:17 and Acts 16:16-40.
34. 2 Corinthians 12:7. We do not know whether this "thorn" refers to a persistent illness or disorder.
35. See 2 Corinthians 12:9.
36. See Acts 7:54-60.
37. See and cf. Matthew 26:39-42, Mark 14:32-39, and Luke 22:39-46. The account of Jesus praying in the Garden of Gethsemane is not recorded in John.
38. This practice may be reflected in James 5:14-16.
39. Morton T. Kelsey, *Healing and Christianity: In Ancient Thought and Modern Times* (New York: Harper and Row, 1973), 179-80.
40. Robin Gill, *A Textbook of Christian Ethics* (Edinburgh: T. & T. Clark, 1985), 430.
41. Kenneth L. Vaux, *Death Ethics: Religious and Cultural Values in Prolonging and Ending Life* (Philadelphia: Trinity Press International, 1992), 40.
42. Jerry B. Wilson, *Death by Decision: The Medical, Moral, and Legal Dilemmas of Euthanasia* (Philadelphia: Westminster Press, 1975), 26.
43. As quoted in Kelsey, *Healing and Christianity*, 208.
44. Ibid., 209.
45. Wilson, *Death by Decision*, 26.
46. As quoted in Wilson, *Death by Decision*, 26.
47. Wilson, *Death by Decision*, 24.
48. Vaux, *Death Ethics*, 49.
49. As quoted in Vaux, *Death Ethics*, 49.
50. It is also interesting to note that Hume argued that belief in divine providence or predestination might include acts of suicide. Consequently, opposing a right to commit suicide might mean opposing the will of God.
51. "Selections from the Hippocratic Corpus," in *Ethics in Medicine: Historical Perspectives and Contemporary Concerns*, ed. Stanley Joel Reiser, Arthur J. Dyck, and William J. Curran (Cambridge: MIT Press, 1977), 5.
52. As quoted in Wilson, *Death by Decision*, 27.
53. Wilson, *Death by Decision*, 27.
54. As quoted in Wilson, *Death by Decision*, 27.
55. As quoted in Vaux, *Death Ethics*, 41.
56. As quoted in Vaux, *Death Ethics*, 48.

3. Theological Themes

1. Arthur Peacocke, *Theology for a Scientific Age: Being and Becoming — Natural and Divine* (Oxford: Basil Blackwell, 1990), 105.

2. Colin E. Gunton, *Christ and Creation* (Carlisle, U.K.: Paternoster Press, 1992), 74.
3. Ibid., 37.
4. See, for example, Leviticus 25.
5. Isaiah 42:6 and 49:6.
6. Isaiah 49:6.
7. See Romans 8:18-23.
8. See 1 Corinthians 12.
9. 2 Corinthians 5:17.
10. Peacocke, *Theology for a Scientific Age*, 62-63.
11. Isaiah 45:7.
12. Romans 14:9.
13. John Polkinghorne, *Science and Providence: God's Interaction with the World* (London: SPCK, 1989), 40.
14. Ibid., 43.
15. Ibid., 43.
16. Ibid., 17.
17. Genesis 14:18.
18. See Matthew 10:38.
19. Genesis 1:22. See also v. 28.
20. Claus Westermann, *Genesis 1-11: A Commentary*, trans. John J. Scullion (London: SPCK, 1984), 140.
21. John F. Kilner, *Life on the Line: Ethics, Aging, Ending Patients' Lives, and Allocating Vital Resources* (Grand Rapids, Mich.: Wm. B. Eerdmans, 1992), 67.
22. Gunton, *Christ and Creation*, 45.
23. Ibid., 46.
24. See Romans 12:2 and Philippians 3:21.
25. Gunton, *Christ and Creation*, 45.
26. See John 3:17-21.
27. John 3:3.
28. 1 Peter 2:5.
29. 2 Corinthians 5:17.
30. Romans 12:1.
31. Romans 8:19.
32. Romans 8:20 ; see also 8:18-23.
33. Oliver O'Donovan, *Resurrection and Moral Order: An Outline for Evangelical Ethics* (Grand Rapids, Mich.: Wm. B. Eerdmans, 1986), 55.
34. James D. G. Dunn, *Romans 1-8* (Dallas: Word Books, 1988), 471.
35. Gunton, *Christ and Creation*, 97.
36. Romans 8:23.
37. Polkinghorne, *Science and Providence*, 70.
38. Ibid., 73-74.
39. From the hymn "Amazing Grace."
40. Kilner, *Life on the Line*, 103.

41. Isaiah 53:5.
42. Kilner, *Life on the Line*, 107.
43. Ibid., 101-2.
44. Stanley Hauerwas, with Richard Bondi and David B. Burrell, *Truthfulness and Tragedy: Further Investigations in Christian Ethics* (Notre Dame, Ind.: University of Notre Dame Press, 1977), 168.
45. Galatians 1:4.
46. O'Donovan, *Resurrection and Moral Order*, 95.
47. Vaux, *Death Ethics*, 128.
48. See Genesis 3:19-22.
49. 1 Corinthians 15:56.
50. 1 Corinthians 15:22.
51. 1 Corinthians 15:21.
52. Augustine, *The City of God*, vol. 1, trans. Marcus Dods (Edinburgh: T. & T. Clark, 1872), 523.
53. Jeremiah 12:1.
54. Ecclesiastes 7:15.
55. Matthew 5:45.
56. Stanley Hauerwas, *The Peaceable Kingdom: A Primer in Christian Ethics* (Notre Dame, Ind.: University of Notre Dame Press, 1983), 105.
57. 1 Corinthians 15:26.
58. 1 Corinthians 15:54.
59. 1 Corinthians 15:55.
60. Augustine, *City of God*, 522-23.
61. Ibid., 257.
62. Ecclesiastes 3:2.
63. Wennberg, *Terminal Choices*, 70.
64. Kilner, *Life on the Line*, 103.
65. Hauerwas, *Truthfulness and Tragedy*, 111.
66. Ibid.
67. Romans 6:5.
68. Romans 8:25.
69. O'Donovan, *Resurrection and Moral Order*, 247.
70. See 1 Corinthians 15:20-28.
71. O'Donovan, *Resurrection and Moral Order*, 249.
72. See John Macquarrie, *Christian Hope* (New York: Seabury Press, 1978).
73. Polkinghorne, *Science and Providence*, 97.
74. See Oscar Cullmann, *Immortality of the Soul or Resurrection of the Dead? The Witness of the New Testament* (London: Epworth Press, 1958).
75. Polkinghorne, *Science and Providence*, 90.
76. Ibid., 89.
77. Ibid., 90.
78. 1 Corinthians 15:22.

79. 1 Corinthians 13:12 (NEB).
80. Polkinghorne, *Science and Providence*, 90.

4. Approaches to Moral Reflection and Discernment

1. See Alasdair MacIntyre, *After Virtue* (Notre Dame, Ind.: University of Notre Dame Press, 1981); see also Brent Waters and Rob Stuart, "Being Good and Being Reasonable," *Theology Today* 50:3 (October 1993), 358-72.
2. Keith Berndtson, "Mandatory HIV Testing and the Character of Medicine," *Second Opinion* 19:3 (January 1994), 27.
3. See Stanley Hauerwas, *Against the Nations: War and Survival in a Liberal Society* (Notre Dame, Ind.: University of Notre Dame Press, 1992), 23-50.
4. Ruth Macklin, *Mortal Choices: Ethical Dilemmas in Modern Medicine* (Boston: Houghton Mifflin, 1987), 168.
5. Macklin, *Mortal Choices*, 168.
6. See Tom L. Beauchamp and James F. Childress, *Principles of Biomedical Ethics* (New York: Oxford University Press, 1979); cf. H. Tristram Engelhardt Jr., *The Foundations of Bioethics* (New York: Oxford University Press, 1986).
7. Ibid., 56.
8. Ibid., 98-102.
9. Ibid., 136.
10. Ibid., 169.
11. Gill, *Christian Ethics*, 6.
12. Macklin, *Mortal Choices*, 31.
13. Gill, *Christian Ethics*, 7.
14. Beauchamp and Childress, *Principles of Biomedical Ethics*, 22.
15. For additional readings in deontological and teleological ethics, see Appendix 3.
16. Ronald M. Green, Bernard Gert, and K. Danner Clouser, "The Method of Public Morality Versus the Method of Principlism," *Journal of Medicine and Philosophy* 18:5 (October 1993): 484.
17. Ibid., 483.
18. Hauerwas, *Truthfulness and Tragedy*, 23.
19. Stanley Hauerwas, *A Community of Character: Toward a Constructive Christian Social Ethic* (Notre Dame, Ind.: University of Notre Dame Press, 1981), 9.
20. See Carol Gilligan, *In a Different Voice: Psychological Theory and Women's Development* (Cambridge: Harvard University Press, 1982).
21. See Aristotle's *Nicomachean Ethics*.
22. George W. Stroup, *The Promise of Narrative Theology: Recovering the Gospel in the Church* (Atlanta: John Knox Press, 1981), 92.

23. Hauerwas, *Truthfulness and Tragedy*, 36.
24. See James W. McClendon Jr., *Ethics: Systematic Theology*, vol. 1 (Nashville: Abingdon Press, 1986); Robert W. Jenson, "How the World Lost Its Story," *First Things* 36 (October 1993): 19-24; and John H. Yoder, *The Politics of Jesus* (Grand Rapids, Mich.: Wm. B. Eerdmans, 1972).
25. H. Richard Niebuhr, *The Responsible Self: An Essay in Christian Moral Philosophy* (New York: Harper and Row, 1963), 67.
26. Beauchamp and Childress, *Biomedical Ethics*, 233.
27. Howard Brody, " The Physician/Patient Relationship," in *Medical Ethics*, ed. Robert M. Veatch (Boston: Jones and Bartlett, 1989), 77.
28. See Robert Coles, *The Call of Stories: Teaching and Moral Imagination* (Boston: Houghton Mifflin, 1989).
29. See Hauerwas, *Suffering Presence*, 23-83; cf. May, *Physician's Covenant*, 106-92.
30. Englehardt, *Foundations of Bioethics*, 53.
31. Albert R. Jonsen and Stephen Toulmin, *The Abuse of Casuistry: A History of Moral Reasoning* (Berkeley: University of California Press, 1988), 13.
32. Ibid., 13.
33. See Stephen Toulmin, "The Recovery of Practical Philosophy," *The American Scholar* 57:3 (summer 1988): 337-51.
34. Jonsen and Toulmin, *Abuse of Casuistry*, 11.
35. Ibid., 13.
36. Ibid.
37. Ibid., 343.
38. Ibid., 17.
39. Ibid., 18.
40. Ibid.
41. Ibid.
42. See Edward Shils, "The Sanctity of Life," in *Life or Death: Ethics and Options* (Portland, Oreg.: Reed College, 1964), 2-38.
43. Ibid., 12.
44. Ibid., 12.
45. The problem is determining what constitutes "nature's course" or when the "divinely appointed hour" has arrived.
46. Vigen Guroian, "Death and Dying Well in the Orthodox Liturgical Tradition," *Second Opinion* 19:1 (July 1993): 53.
47. Ibid., 55.
48. Shils, "Sanctity of Life," 37.
49. James J. Walter and Thomas A. Shannon, foreword to *Quality of Life*, ed. Walter and Shannon, 2.
50. For example, see Karl Barth, *Ethics*, 126-28.
51. Richard A. McCormick, "To Save or Let Die," in *Quality of Life*, ed. Walter and Shannon, 32.

52. James Rachels, *The End of Life: Euthanasia and Morality* (Oxford: Oxford University Press, 1986).
53. Ibid., 64.
54. Ibid.
55. Ibid., 65.
56. The Hastings Center Staff, "Quality of Life," in *Quality of Life*, ed. Walter and Shannon, 326.
57. For additional readings reflecting sanctity of life and quality of life considerations, see Appendix 3.

5. Moral Questions Raised by Dying and Death

1. To date, only the Netherlands permits active euthanasia.
2. For a summary of ethical concerns relating to proposals for more "liberal" euthanasia laws, see Albert R. Jonsen, "Living With Euthanasia: A Futuristic Scenario," *Journal of Medicine and Philosophy* 18:3 (June 1993): 241-51.
3. See E. Haavi Morreim, "Profoundly Diminished Life: The Casualties of Coercion," *Hastings Center Report* 24:1 (January-February 1994): 33-42.
4. See Ronald Cole-Turner, *The New Genesis: Theology and the Genetic Revolution* (Louisville: Westminster John Knox, 1993).
5. See Troy Duster, *Backdoor to Eugenics* (New York: Routledge, 1990); cf. Jean Bethke Elshtain, "The New Eugenics and Feminist Quandaries: Philosophical and Political Reflections," in *Guaranteeing the Good Life: Medicine and the Return of Eugenics*, ed. Richard John Neuhaus (Grand Rapids, Mich.: Wm. B. Eerdmans, 1990), 68-88.
6. For example, see Hauerwas, *Suffering Presence*, 159-81.
7. Colin E. Gunton, *The One, the Three, and the Many: God, Creation, and the Culture of Modernity: The Bampton Lectures, 1992* (Cambridge: Cambridge University Press, 1993), 38.

6. Epilogue

1. Barth, *Ethics*, 196.
2. Hauerwas, *Truthfulness and Tragedy*, 108.
3. See Stanley Hauerwas, *Naming the Silences: God, Medicine, and the Problem of Suffering* (Grand Rapids, Mich.: Wm. B. Eerdmans, 1990).
4. Vaux, *Death Ethics*, 44.
5. Paul S. Fiddes, *The Creative Suffering of God* (Oxford: Clarendon Press, 1988), 16.
6. 1 Corinthians 13:12 (NEB).

7. Fiddes, *Creative Suffering*, 267.
8. From the hymn "Love Divine, All Loves Excelling."
9. As quoted in Thomas Merton, *Mystics and Zen Masters* (New York: Delta Books, 1967), 144.
10. From the hymn "Love Divine, All Loves Excelling."

Bibliography

Albright, W. F., and C. S. Mann. *Matthew*. Garden City, N.Y.: Doubleday, 1971.
Augustine. *The City of God*. Translated by Marcus Dods. Edinburgh: T. & T. Clark, 1872.
Barth, Karl. *Ethics*. Edited by Dietrich Braun. Translated by Geoffrey Bromiley. New York: Seabury Press, 1981.
Beauchamp, Tom L., and James F. Childress. *Principles of Biomedical Ethics*. New York: Oxford University Press, 1979.
Berndtson, Keith. "Mandatory HIV Testing and the Character of Medicine." *Second Opinion* 19:3 (1992).
Campbell, Courtney S. "Religious Ethics and Active Euthanasia in a Pluralistic Society." *Kennedy Institute of Ethics Journal* 2:3 (1992).
Coles, Robert. *The Call of Stories: Teaching and Moral Imagination*. Boston: Houghton Mifflin, 1989.
Cole-Turner, Ronald. *The New Genesis: Theology and the Genetic Revolution*. Louisville: Westminster John Knox, 1993.
Cullmann, Oscar. *Immortality of the Soul or Resurrection of the Dead? The Witness of the New Testament*. London: Epworth Press, 1958.
Dunn, James D. G. *Romans 1-8*. Dallas: Word Books, 1988.
Duster, Troy. *Backdoor to Eugenics*. New York: Routledge, 1990.
Engelhardt, H. Tristram, Jr. *The Foundations of Bioethics*. New York: Oxford University Press, 1986.
Fiddes, Paul S. *The Creative Suffering of God*. Oxford: Clarendon Press, 1988.

Gerstenberger, Erhard S., and Wolfgang Schrage. *Suffering*. Translated by John E. Steely. Nashville: Abingdon, 1980.

Gill, Robin. *A Textbook of Christian Ethics*. Edinburgh: T. & T. Clark, 1985.

Gilligan, Carol. *In a Different Voice: Psychological Theory and Women's Development*. Cambridge: Harvard University Press, 1982.

Green, Ronald M., Bernard Gert, and K. Danner Clouser. "The Method of Public Morality versus the Method of Principlism." *Journal of Medicine and Philosophy* 18:5 (1993).

Gunton, Colin E. *Christ and Creation*. Carlisle, U.K.: Paternoster Press, 1992.

―――. *The One, the Three, and the Many: God, Creation, and the Culture of Modernity: The Bampton Lectures, 1992*. Cambridge: Cambridge University Press, 1993.

Guroian, Vigen. "Death and Dying Well in the Orthodox Liturgical Tradition." *Second Opinion* 19:1 (1993).

Hauerwas, Stanley. *Against the Nations: War and Survival in a Liberal Society*. Notre Dame, Ind.: University of Notre Dame Press, 1992.

A Community of Character: Toward a Constructive Christian Social Ethic. Notre Dame, Ind.: University of Notre Dame Press, 1981.

―――. *Naming the Silences: God, Medicine, and the Problem of Suffering*. Grand Rapids, Mich.: Wm. B. Eerdmans, 1990.

―――. *The Peaceable Kingdom: A Primer in Christian Ethics*. Notre Dame, Ind.: University of Notre Dame Press, 1983.

―――. *Suffering Presence: Theological Reflections on Medicine, the Mentally Handicapped, and the Church*. Notre Dame, Ind.: University of Notre Dame Press, 1986.

Hauerwas, Stanley, with Richard Bondi and David B. Burrell. *Truthfulness and Tragedy: Further Investigations in Christian Ethics*. Notre Dame, Ind.: University of Notre Dame Press, 1977.

Hertzberg, Hans Wilhelm. *I and II Samuel: A Commentary*. Translated by J. S. Bowden. Philadelphia: Westminster Press, 1960.

Jenson, Robert W. "How the World Lost Its Story." *First Things* 36 (1993).

Jonsen, Albert R. "Living with Euthanasia: A Futuristic Scenario." *Journal of Medicine and Philosophy* 18:3 (1993).

Jonsen, Albert R., and Stephen Toulmin. *The Abuse of Casuistry: A History of Moral Reasoning*. Berkeley: University of California Press, 1988.

Kelsey, Morton T. *Healing and Christianity: In Ancient Thought and Modern Times*. New York: Harper and Row, 1973.

Kilner, John F. *Life on the Line: Ethics, Aging, Ending Patients' Lives, and Allocating Vital Resources*. Grand Rapids, Mich.: Wm. B. Eerdmans, 1992.

MacIntyre, Alasdair. *After Virtue: A Study in Moral Theory*. 2d ed. Notre Dame, Ind.: University of Notre Dame Press, 1984.

Macklin, Ruth. *Mortal Choices: Ethical Dilemmas in Modern Medicine*. Boston: Houghton Mifflin, 1987.

Macquarrie, John. *Christian Hope*. New York: Seabury Press, 1978.

May, William F. *The Physician's Covenant: Images of the Healer in Medical Ethics*. Philadelphia: Westminster Press, 1983.

McClendon, James Wm., Jr. *Ethics: Systematic Theology*. Vol 1. Nashville: Abingdon Press, 1986.

Merton, Thomas. *Mystics and Zen Masters*. New York: Delta Books, 1967.

Morreim, E. Haavi. "Profoundly Diminished Life: The Casualties of Coercion." *Hastings Center Report* 24:1 (1994).

Munck, Johannes. *The Acts of the Apostles*. Garden City, N.Y.: Doubleday, 1967.

Neuhaus, Richard John, ed. *Guaranteeing the Good Life: Medicine and the Return of Eugenics*. Grand Rapids, Mich.: Wm. B. Eerdmans, 1990.

Niebuhr, H. Richard. *The Responsible Self: An Essay in Christian Moral Philosophy*. New York: Harper and Row, 1963.

O'Donovan, Oliver. *Resurrection and Moral Order: An Outline for Evangelical Ethics*. Grand Rapids, Mich.: Wm. B. Eerdmans, 1986.

Peacocke, Arthur. *Theology for a Scientific Age: Being and Becoming—Natural and Divine*. Oxford: Basil Blackwell, 1990.

Polkinghorne, John. *Science and Providence: God's Interaction with the World*. London: SPCK, 1989.

Rachels, James. *The End of Life: Euthanasia and Morality*. Oxford: Oxford University Press, 1986.

Ramsey, Paul. *The Patient as Person: Explorations in Medical Ethics*. New Haven: Yale University Press, 1970.

Reiser, Stanley Joel, Arthur J. Dyck, and William J. Curran, eds. *Ethics in Medicine: Historical Perspectives and Contemporary Concerns*. Cambridge: MIT Press, 1977.

Stroup, George W. *The Promise of Narrative Theology: Recovering the Gospel in the Church*. Atlanta: John Knox Press, 1981.

Thomasma, David C., and Glenn C. Graber. *Euthanasia: Toward an Ethical Social Policy*. New York: Continuum, 1991.

Toulmin, Stephen. "The Recovery of Practical Philosophy." *The American Scholar* 57:3 (1988).

Vaux, Kenneth L. *Death Ethics: Religious and Cultural Values in Prolonging and Ending Life*. Philadelphia: Trinity Press International, 1992.

Veatch, Robert M. *Medical Ethics*. Boston: Jones and Bartlett, 1989.

Walter, James J., and Thomas A. Shannon, eds. *Quality of Life: The New Medical Dilemma*. New York: Paulist Press, 1990.

Waters, Brent, and Rob Stuart. "Being Good and Being Reasonable." *Theology Today* 50:3 (1993).

Wennberg, Robert N. *Terminal Choices: Euthanasia, Suicide, and the Right to Die*. Grand Rapids, Mich.: Wm. B. Eerdmans, 1989.

Westermann, Claus. *Genesis 1-11: A Commentary*. Translated by John J. Scullion. London: SPCK, 1984.

Wilson, Jerry B. *Death by Decision: The Medical, Moral, and Legal Dilemmas of Euthanasia*. Philadelphia: Westminster Press, 1975.

Yoder, John H. *The Politics of Jesus*. Grand Rapids, Mich.: Wm. B. Eerdmans, 1972.

Index

Abimelech, 29-30
access to medical treatment, 95-100
active euthanasia, 12, 38-39, 89, 92
advance directive, 88, 90, 123
age, and access to treatment, 96
Ahithophel, 29-30
AIDS, 4, 110-11
Alzheimer's disease, 4-5, 111-12
Apostolic Constitutions, 31
Aristotle, 65, 74
Augustine, 31-32, 54, 57
autonomy, 13-14, 68, 82, 89, 123

Bacon, Francis, 34
Barth, Karl, 29, 107
Beauchamp, Tom L., 68
beneficence, 68, 89, 123
Bentham, Jeremy, 35, 70
Berndtson, Keith, 65
bioethics, 66, 123; deontological ethics and, 68-69; medical school instruction, 75; moral casuistry and, 77-79; narrative ethics and, 75-76; teleological ethics and, 71-72. *See also* ethics
brain death, 8-9, 123

Campbell, Courtney S., 16
care of sick and dying, 113-14; biblical attitudes, 27-28; early church attitudes, 31; ministry of healing, 31, 33, 34-35, 113; personal factors and, 95-100
case studies. *See* moral casuistry
casuistry. *See* moral casuistry
Childress, James F., 68
chronic disease, and access to treatment, 98
church: faith of, 21-22; reflection on death, 20
City of God (Augustine), 31
Coffin, Henry Sloane, 36
compassion, 56, 114
consequentialist ethics. *See* teleological ethics
Council of Trent, 33
creation, redemption of, 47-54

Darwin, Charles, 36-37
death: acceptance of, 109-10; as avoidance or relief from suffering, 30-31; definitions of, 8-9; determining occurrence of, 8-9; doxology of, 107-16; as friend versus

death (*cont.*)
  enemy, 57-58; responses to, 9-10; theological themes, 57-61; tragedy of, 109. *See also* dying and death
death with dignity, 55-56, 90-91
deontological ethics, 67-69, 124; bioethics and, 68-69; physician-assisted suicide and, 93; quality of life and, 82; sanctity of life and, 80
disabled patient, 93-94
disease, response to, 9-10
doctors. *See* health care professionals
Donne, John, 33
doxology of death, 107-16
dying, care of. *See* care of sick and dying
dying and death: AIDS patient, 4, 110-11; Alzheimer's disease, 4-5, 111-12; biblical attitudes, 27-31; changing attitudes, 6-8; contemporary Christian attitudes, 37-40; early church attitudes, 31-32; elderly patient, 3-4, 110; faith of the church, 21-22; God as source of, 43-45; hospital deaths, 7; medieval church attitudes, 32-33; modern Christian attitudes, 35-37; reflection on, 16-20; Reformist attitudes, 33-35; single adult, 4-5, 111-12; spouse, 5-6, 112-13; suffering and, 54-57; theological significance of, 20-22; theological traditions, 21; young adult, 4, 110-11. *See also* care of sick and dying; death

Engelhardt, H. Tristram, Jr., 76
ethics, 65-67; deontological, 67-69, 124; medical school instruction, 75; narrative, 73-76, 91, 124-25; teleological, 69-73, 126. *See also* bioethics
ethics of character. *See* narrative ethics

eugenics, 12, 37, 97
euthanasia, 12-16, 124; active, 12, 38-39, 89, 92; advocacy groups, 36; autonomy and, 13-14; contemporary Christian attitudes, 38-39; early church attitudes, 31; informed consent and, 13-14; involuntary, 12, 34, 38; medieval church attitudes, 32; modern Christian attitudes, 35-37; moral decisions, 88-91; nonvoluntary, 12, 38-39; passive, 12, 38-39, 92; for patients not terminally ill, 13-14; physician-assisted suicide compared with, 91-92; physician reflection on, 36; Reformist attitudes, 33-34; suicide compared with, 14; surrogate decision-maker, 13, 88, 125; voluntary, 12, 33-34, 38-39. *See also* physician-assisted suicide
Euthanasia Society, 36
evolutionary theory, 36-37
extreme unction, sacrament of, 33, 34

family, reflection on death, 17
Fosdick, Harry Emerson, 36
friends, reflection on death, 17-18

genetics, 36-37, 97
God: as creator, 41-42; as healer, 42-43; as personal God, 44-45; as redeemer, 42-43; as source of suffering and death, 43-45; as sustenance, 43; theological themes, 41-45
Graber, Glenn C., 7
grief, 58-59
Gunton, Colin E., 42, 46-47, 102

Hartlib, Samuel, 34
Hastings Center, 83
Hauerwas, Stanley, 51, 55, 74-75, 108-9

Index

healing: medical practice and, 10; ministry of, 31, 33, 34-35, 113; as redemption, 42-43, 48-50
health care. *See* medical treatment; medicine
health care institutions: conflicts of interest, 19-20; deaths in, 7; reflection on death, 19-20; responsibilities of, 19-20
health care professionals: ethics instruction, 75; reflection on death, 18-19; reflection on euthanasia, 36; relationship with patients, 18-19, 69, 75; values of, 11
health care reform, 95
Hippocratic oath, 14, 36, 37-38
"Holy Hammer," 32
hope, 59-61, 115
hospice, 124
Hume, David, 35

incompetent patient, 11, 87, 90, 124
informed consent, 13-14, 124
institutions. *See* health care institutions
involuntary euthanasia, 12, 34, 38
Isaiah, 43, 50-51

Jesus, 31, 51, 52
Job, 28, 30
Jonah, 30
Jonsen, Albert, 77-78
Judas Iscariot, 29-30
Julian of Norwich, 116
justice, 68

Kant, Immanuel, 65, 67-68
Kevorkian, Jack, 14, 91
Kilner, John F., 45, 51, 58

last rites, 33, 34
life: as gift and loan from God, 32, 45-47, 108, 111; psychosomatic unity of, 60; quality of life perspective, 15, 38, 81-83, 88, 93-94, 125; sanctity of life perspective, 15, 38, 79-81, 88, 125; stewardship of, 46-47, 111-12; storylike structure of, 74-75; theological themes, 45-47; value of, 15
life-prolonging treatment, 7-8, 55, 90-91, 99, 110, 124
lifestyles, and access to treatment, 98-99
Luther, Martin, 34

Macklin, Ruth, 68, 70
Macquarrie, John, 60
martyrdom, 32-33
Marx, Carl F. H., 36
May, William F., 9
medical research, 78
medical treatment: access to, 95-100; costs, 10, 19, 95; life-prolonging, 7-8, 55, 90-91, 99, 110, 124; medieval church attitudes, 33; technological advances, 7-8, 35-36, 83; withholding/withdrawing, 11-12, 38-39, 86-88, 91-92, 126. *See also* health care institutions; health care professionals
medicine: contemporary practice of, 9-11; healing and, 10; health care reform, 95; as moral community, 58, 75-76, 111-12; moral practice of, 68-69, 75-76; teleological ethics and, 72. *See also* health care institutions; health care professionals
mental retardation, 99-100
mercy killing. *See* euthanasia
metanoia, 47-48
Mill, John Stuart, 70
ministry: of healing, 31, 33, 34-35, 113; redemptive nature of, 52-53
moral casuistry, 76-79, 123-24; bioethics and, 77-79; quality of

moral casuistry (*cont.*)
  life and, 82-83; sanctity of life
  and, 80
moral duties. *See* deontological
  ethics
morality, defined, 75
moral reflection and discernment,
  63, 65-67, 85-86; masculine versus feminist approaches, 74, 79.
  See also ethics; moral casuistry;
  quality of life; sanctity of life
moral taxonomies. *See* moral
  casuistry
More, Thomas, 33-34

Naaman, 28
narrative ethics, 73-76, 91, 124-25;
  bioethics and, 75-76; physician-assisted suicide and, 93; quality of
  life and, 82; sanctity of life and, 80
National Commission for the Protection of Human Subjects of Biomedical and Behavioral Research, 78
Nazi regime, 12, 37
Newton, John, 50
nonmaleficence, 68, 125
nonvoluntary euthanasia, 12, 38-39

pain. *See* suffering
Pascal, Blaise, 77
passive euthanasia, 12, 38-39, 92
pastoral care, 20, 35
Paul: on healing, 43; on hope, 59, 60,
  115; on redemption, 48; response
  to suffering, 30; on sin, 54, 57
Percy, Walker, 81, 83
persistent vegetative state, 5-6, 12,
  19-20, 112-13, 125
personal reflection on death, 16
petitionary prayer, 49-50, 53
physician-assisted suicide, 14-15,
  37-38, 91-95, 125; deontological
  ethics and, 93; euthanasia compared with, 91-92; narrative ethics and, 93; teleological ethics and,

93; withholding medical treatment
  compared with, 91-92. *See also*
  euthanasia
physician-patient relationship, 18-
  19, 69, 75
physicians. *See* health care professionals
Plato, 60
Polkinghorne, John, 44, 49-50, 60,
  61
pragmatism, 70
prayer, petitionary, 49-50, 53
psychosomatic unity of life, 60
public policies, 78-79

quality of life, 15, 38, 81-83, 88,
  93-94, 125; deontological ethics
  and, 82; moral casuistry and, 82-
  83; narrative ethics and, 82; teleological ethics and, 82
Quill, Timothy, 14

Rachels, James, 82
redemption, 42; of creation, 47-54;
  healing as, 42-43, 48-50; ministry
  as, 52-53; suffering as, 50-52
reflection, levels of, 16-20; church,
  20; family, 17; friends, 17-18;
  health care professionals, 18-19;
  institutions, 19-20; personal, 16;
  theological, 20-22
Reformers, attitudes toward death,
  33-35
Resolution on Rights and Responsibilities of Christians Regarding Human Death, 117-21
resurrection, 59-60, 115
Rights and Responsibilities of Christians Regarding Human Death,
  The, 117-21
right to die, 90-91

salvation. *See* redemption
sanctity of life, 15, 38, 79-81, 88,
  125; deontological ethics and, 80;

moral casuistry and, 80; narrative ethics and, 80; teleological ethics and, 80
Saul, 29-30
selective breeding, 36-37
Sheol, 60
sick, care of. *See* care of sick and dying
sin, 47-48; suffering and, 54-57
situational ethics. *See* moral casuistry
Social Darwinism, 37
Stephen, 30
stewardship of life, 46-47, 111-12
storylike structure of life, 74-75
suffering, 35-36; biblical attitudes, 28-31; contemporary Christian attitudes, 39-40; death as avoidance or relief from, 30-31; dying and, 54-57; early church attitudes, 31-32; for others, 51-53; God as source of, 43-45; medieval church attitudes, 32-33; redemptive nature of, 50-52; Reformist attitudes, 33; sin and, 54-57; theology and, 54-57; with others, 51-53
suicide: biblical attitudes, 29-30; contemporary Christian attitudes, 37-38; early church attitudes, 31; euthanasia compared with, 14; medieval church attitudes, 32; modern Christian attitudes, 35; physician-assisted, 14-15, 37-38, 91-95, 125; prevention of, 14; Reformist attitudes, 33
surrogate, 13, 88, 125

Table Talk (Luther), 34
teleological ethics, 69-73, 126; bioethics and, 71-72; physician-assisted suicide and, 93; practice of medicine and, 72; quality of life and, 82; sanctity of life and, 80
terminal disease, and access to treatment, 96, 97, 98
Thanatos Syndrome, The (Percy), 81, 83
theological reflection, 20-22
theological themes: death, 57-61; God, 41-45; life, 45-47; redemption of creation, 47-54; suffering and dying, 54-57
theology, 25, 41, 61
Thomasma, David C., 7
Toulmin, Stephen, 77-78
transplants, 8

utilitarianism, 70
Utopia (More), 33-34

Vaux, Kenneth, 32, 113-14
virtue ethics. *See* narrative ethics
voluntary euthanasia, 12, 33-34, 38-39
voluntary lifestyles, and access to treatment, 98-99

Wennberg, Robert, 29-30, 57
Wesley, Charles, 115-16
Williams, S. D., Jr., 36
withholding/withdrawing medical treatment, 11-12, 38-39, 86-88, 126; physician-assisted suicide compared with, 91-92
worship, 114-15

Zimri, 29-30